CULTS
COERCION AND CONTROL

The World's Most Notorious Cults
(And The People Who Escaped Them)

JAMIE KING

summersdale

CULTS: COERCION AND CONTROL

Text by Zoe Apostolides

An Hachette UK Company
www.hachette.co.uk

Summersdale Publishers
Part of Octopus Publishing Group Limited
Carmelite House
50 Victoria Embankment
LONDON
EC4Y 0DZ
UK

www.summersdale.com

Printed and bound in the UK

ISBN: 978-1-83799-280-5

Substantial discounts on bulk quantities of Summersdale books are available to corporations, professional associations and other organizations. For details contact general enquiries: telephone: +44 (0) 1243 771107 or email: enquiries@summersdale.com.

Disclaimer
All the stories in the book have been at some point expressed in the public domain. Every effort has been made to ensure that all information is correct. Should there be any errors, we apologize and shall be pleased to make the appropriate amendments in any future editions.

CONTENTS

INTRODUCTION

For as long as there have been societal norms, there have been groups keen to break away from them. In all corners of the world and right across the breadth of time, groups and sects – as well as branches of established religions – have welcomed members who feel, for myriad different reasons, that contemporary life and its conventional trappings are somehow unsatisfactory.

From earliest youth, many children long to be part of a gang, a club, an exclusive organization that identifies itself in opposition to the other. This drive for comfort gained from a sense of shared purpose can be just as alluring to adults, particularly those on society's fringes. It is into this void, this deep desire for connection, that the cult – with all its rhetoric, its focus on belonging and undivided loyalty, the apparent simplicity of life as described by its many disparate leaders – is born.

For some of the cults described in this book, a fleeting glance would tell the casual observer nothing at all. Part of the enduring fascination with such groups is the fact that, so often, nobody would guess that they might live on an armed compound, having given all their money to an often enigmatic, seemingly benevolent, omnipotent leader. It is this closeness, this passing likeness to "the ordinary" that makes cults across the ages so uncanny.

What, then, might lead a person into a cult? The twentieth century experienced a vast proliferation of new branches, sects and organizations that could, to greater and lesser extents, be classed as "cultish". Cults thrive wherever there is societal change, it seems, or war, poverty, political strife, hardship and hatred. It is little wonder that members of the Leopard Society of Sierra Leone (see page 207) thrived during the height of British colonial rule when the lives of native people were so regimented and controlled. Similarly, the endemic poverty and economic issues prevalent across North and South Korea in the twentieth century, from Japanese rule in the first part to civil war in the second, provided a fertile breeding ground for new groups that promised hope and salvation in an increasingly fraught environment.

Cults come in many stripes, and this book will examine various branches of belief and how these beliefs governed distinct groups. Chapters here will cover everything from religious to political, racist and terrorist cults, from the destructive to the doomsday cult, and will feature well-documented cases and less well-known ones: occasionally, of course, the definitions will overlap when one "genre" of cult appears closely aligned with multiple specific sets of beliefs.

Cults are, by their nature, hard to define. The word comes from the Latin *cultus*, meaning care or worship. In popular culture, cults are synonymous with a group of people believing in something, or someone, or both, often to the exclusion of or in opposition to prescribed ideals and accepted realities. Cults can be spiritual, atheistic or deeply religious across a spectrum of faiths; they might venerate an object, a set of texts or lectures or a specific model of living free from the attachments, distractions and communicative abilities of our modern lives. Often they live isolated from mainstream society and ostensibly advocate for purity or polygamy, Satanism, self-improvement, the existence of extraterrestrials, the End Times, Christ's Second Coming or the supremacy of one race over another.

We might also discuss certain films, books or other forms of popular culture as having a "cult following". This suggests a core and dedicated fan base of the work in question, though it does not – unlike many of the stories in this book – suggest any nefarious or disturbing activity on the part of followers. For many, particularly young people, the reality of true cultism and the total subservience of one's life, family, work, possessions and even self to another "higher" power is a faraway and unimaginable concept.

During the fifth century, in the early Christian Church after the fall of the Roman Empire, Anglo-Saxon society developed a new system of religious beliefs known as the cult of the saints. It was believed that the bones of martyrs could bring forth miracles, demonstrations of the link between heaven and earth. The cult would develop to become a central religious belief system in Western Europe, heralding the dawn of Christianity and replacing the long-held paganism that had been dominant across the British Isles.

The movement accelerated throughout the centuries. Followers grew over time and expanded in line with religious persecution. When a victim was killed for their Christian beliefs, a number of relics would accompany the funerary rites along with tombs, shrines and pilgrimages. When followers needed guidance, cures for illness or family troubles, they would petition the saints, who were held as exemplars of the true faith. Their bodily remains were of the utmost importance, being the last direct link with the corporal body. Churches were constructed in their names, along with paintings and sculptures depicting certain events or scenes from their lives.

Interestingly, both Christianity and Islam were regarded as cults before they became established religions. This legitimization of contemporary new sects continues to occur or not, depending on the nature of a new religion or the branch of an established one, to this day.

Most people studying the phenomenon of cults agree that they usually involve a "parent" religion from which members have deviated in some way – there are clear similarities between Hinduism and the Hare Krishnas, for example, or between Christianity and Korea's Unification Church. When new cults stemming from these origins develop, members are often given a sense from their leader that theirs is the "true" religion or the most accurate interpretation of the parent religion's texts and belief structure.

Many such cults are accused of manipulating existing scriptures to adapt to their own philosophies. In some ways, this seeming adherence to established rites and beliefs can make certain cults particularly hard to identify.

One crucial difference is that recognized organizations usually seek financial help from members to fund their mission and community outreach work, while adherents of cults are usually asked to pay money that's funnelled directly to the leader for personal use. In addition, formalized religions are often transparent and open in their teachings and rules, in contrast to some religious cults, who obfuscate the nature of their belief structure. There is often a hierarchical structure to cults, different to that between priests or imams and their congregations – again, these initiations usually depend on the amount of money "donated".

INTRODUCTION

As these stories will reveal, cult leaders usually react negatively to any questioning or criticism of their beliefs, while most established groups or religions actively encourage debate and discussion. Many victims have been unable to query any actions undertaken by the leader, and have then been barred from leaving the cult altogether.

Many of the former sanctuaries in this book become prisons – and often to the detriment of the finances, dignity, livelihoods or even lives of those who have given everything to belong to the cult in question. And tragically, all too often those prisons prove utterly inescapable.

The stories presented in this book capture the arc of different types of cult around the world and across time. Some seem eccentric, bizarre and even ludicrous, but others are far darker: unsettling, disturbing and, in the worst cases, even deadly. These tales will lift the lid on those sinister leaders and haunting, headline-making cases, showing why an ordinary person can be pulled into something they could never have imagined.

RELIGIOUS CULTS

Many of the religious cults described in the pages that follow have disturbing trajectories, often involving bloodshed, abuse and murder. Their stories are those of victims in thrall to new religions and orthodoxies, of dangerous propaganda and a world view that becomes increasingly at odds with that of society at large. They represent the immense power of groupthink, of brainwashing and of fanaticism. And, more importantly, they seem to be on the rise.

Religious cults have many of the same characteristics as traditional faith movements: believers regard themselves as disciples or followers. Separating religious cults from traditional faith movements or other "genres" of cult described in these pages isn't always easy. Believers will often adhere to a set of agreed principles and ideas. They may regard their leader as a representative of God's will on Earth – whether they are an imam, a rabbi, a priest or guru.

This chapter will examine the origins of various religious cults from around the world and across time. Here we will dive into the social contexts of the eras in which such cults were formed, how they developed and what their followers believed. It is important to note that the first cults described as such – those appearing during Roman times – were in fact religious.

To qualify as a religious cult, new ideologies must be both invented and subsequently accepted by followers. They usually revolve around a single, often charismatic leader. They are different from sects, which usually evolve from a pre-established religious ideology and become "denominations" of that overarching faith. Religious cults, by contrast, rely more heavily on isolated communal living outside the prescribed norms, a strict set of doctrines that tend to involve financial or sexual manipulation, and on experiencing divinity, often through supernatural or directly spiritual means.

Mormonism is an interesting example of a religious movement that is regarded by many outside the group as a cult. Alongside the King James Bible, Mormons also follow the Book of Mormon, the Pearl of Great Price and the Doctrine and Covenants. There are 16 million members of this faith group worldwide, and numbers play a part in deciding whether something is an "accepted" religious ideology or a cult, with all the negative associations that word brings. In short, the more members you have, the more likely it is that you will gain legitimacy. Sometimes, that apparent legitimacy can have frightening consequences.

UTOPIA GONE WRONG

When 76-year-old Catherine "Hyacinth" Thrash woke up on the morning of 19 November 1978, she heard nothing. No shouting, no laughter, no snippets of conversation drifting through the open window of the small one-storey hut she shared with her sister Zipporah. She turned over, realizing as she did so that the bed across from her own was empty.

The day before had certainly been dramatic. A congressman had come to visit the settlement and had left with several members of their community. That was the last she'd heard about it – Catherine had decided to stay put while the others gathered with their leader. She was elderly and tired, choosing to remain behind and wait for Zipporah to return. That was, until a gunshot had sounded out across the tall green trees and the otherwise still night, forcing her to duck under the bed to hide. There had been crying, she remembered: loud wails and screams. The noise must have been loud, since Catherine's hearing wasn't what it had been. She had then crawled into her own bed during the night, once it had all finished – whatever it was.

When she woke up the next morning, she was greeted by an unnerving silence. Catherine had never heard a quiet like it. She pushed open the door of the cabin she shared with the others and stepped out into the jungle. All around her stood similar small houses on stilts, designed to protect inhabitants from the snakes. She scanned the scene before her, squinting in the early-morning light.

What she saw would remain with her forever and would come to represent the largest intentional civilian death toll until 11 September 2001. Catherine Thrash didn't know it yet, but she was one of the few survivors of an unthinkable mass tragedy.

The others – people she had considered family, friends, beloved fellow followers of a cause to which she had dedicated the past 20 years of her life – were all gone. They lay before her, tens of them, hundreds, their brightly coloured clothing a stark contrast to the pale grey of their skin, their motionlessness. And that silence, the heavy and now brutally understandable silence.

Although Catherine didn't know it yet, there were 909 lifeless bodies spread out as far as the eye could see. These were the one-time residents of Jonestown, a community created and developed by a once innocuous man, a community brought to an abrupt and hideous end by one of the worst mass suicides ever recorded. Somewhere among them, Catherine knew, would be their leader.

James Warren Jones was born in rural Indiana in 1931. The boy's father, also called James, sustained injuries in a chemical weapons attack during World War One but his military pension didn't cover the family's necessities. The Great Depression worsened the Jones' fortunes and in 1934 they were evicted from their home after failing to pay the mortgage. Family members clubbed together to purchase a shack instead, which had neither plumbing nor electricity. The years that followed saw a steady worsening of the situation: from time to time, they would be forced to forage for food in the forest.

As he grew older the Jones' son, Jim – as he was now known – developed a friendship with the wife of a local pastor, who gave him his first Bible. The Nazarene Church, of which she was a member, had emerged in the United States during the nineteenth century and is a branch of Protestantism from the Wesleyan-Holiness tradition. Jim was captivated by the Church and was soon stating his desire to become a Christian preacher. He attended services across several different local churches every week and was soon performing his own form of worship through mock funerals for dead animals involved in traffic accidents. Churches primarily attended by Black congregants particularly fascinated Jones and he dreamed of diverse religious congregations.

Jones' unusual behaviour, such as his claim that he could fly, his fascination with death, a series of petty thefts and a clear obsession with religion, meant he was largely an outcast at school, with few close friends. He went on to study the lives and works of Stalin, Mao, Marx, Hitler and Gandhi. At the age of 11, he was at the centre of local controversy when he explained the mechanics of sexual reproduction to other children. By the time he reached adolescence, his reputation as an outsider was concrete. In 1945, Jim's parents separated. He moved to live with his mother in Richmond, Indiana, where he started dating a nurse he'd go on to marry in 1949.

By 1952, Jones had committed fully to his dream of becoming a Methodist minister. He also took up membership of the Communist Party and decided that the Church would be an effective way of spreading his word. While Jim's father had been a member of the Indiana Ku Klux Klan, Jim Jones was a fierce supporter of racial integration and went on to adopt three Korean children, a Native American child, a Black child and a white child. His ultimate aim was the creation of a communist community separate from the authority of the government. In 1955, he founded the People's Temple of the Disciples of Christ with the ostensible aim of making society fairer, and healing people through faith.

Seven years later, Jim Jones found what he was looking for in an isolated swathe of land in Guyana, which he leased from that country's government and began to clear in preparation for inhabitants. The 3,852-acre plot became the Jonestown Agricultural Settlement but was sparsely populated until around mid-1977.

At this point Jones himself was still based in the United States, until he learned that a group of ex-members had spoken to the press and that an exposé of his cult was due to be published. By the time it was, Jones along with a few hundred followers – many of whom were from impoverished families contacted directly by the leader and who had witnessed his sermons and joint campaigns with other prominent Christian ministers – had flown to Guyana and settled on the compound.

The new community was demographically mixed, with a blend of senior citizens, working-age adults, children and teenagers: the majority of residents were Black, a fact explained by the aftermath – the fear, confusion and grief experienced by these communities all over the country – of Martin Luther King Jr's 1968 assassination and the tide of racial conflict sweeping the United States as a whole.

For many Black Americans, Jonestown represented a fresh start, and Jim Jones' so-called utopia seemed to provide such an environment. Often for the first time in their lives, Black Americans were granted positions of authority and leadership on the Guyana plot. About twice as many women as men lived in Jonestown, with a proportion of 45 per cent Black females, 13 per cent white females and 23 per cent Black males. It is thought likely that Jones' apparent charisma and charm played a key role in attracting the group's female followers.

From the start, the settlement was not quite what its residents had anticipated. There were not enough cabins, leading to overcrowding, and married couples were separated since dormitories were single sex. It was extremely humid and disease spread quickly, a situation exacerbated by the 11 hours' work – mostly agricultural labour – healthy adults were expected to perform each day. Children were generally only permitted to see their parents briefly, at night, and were encouraged to address Jones as "Father" or "Dad". Food was scarce, with some "defectors" describing meagre meals of rice and vegetables or oatmeal.

The monthly Social Security cheques made out to pensioners were cashed in lieu of their ability to work. All day, every day, Jones' voice could be heard throughout the camp, monologuing long into the night. He had become a demagogue, a dictator, and, though some residents marvelled at his rhetoric and ideas, others grew increasingly disenfranchised. The problem was that leaving was near impossible: dense jungle surrounded the community and armed guards were stationed all around.

A group of concerned family members from outside the cult had petitioned a Californian congressman called Leo Ryan to look into the matter. As happens with many cult organizations, these family members had been effectively cut off from their Jonestown relatives and were concerned for their safety. Ryan agreed to make the trip alongside them, all the way to Guyana, and took with him an NBC film crew. The group arrived on 17 November 1978.

For the first few hours of their arrival, Ryan was pleasantly surprised by the situation at Jonestown. It wasn't until dinner that evening that one of the film-crew members was handed a note containing the names of people who wanted to leave. The next day, 18 November, Ryan publicly declared that anybody who wanted to go could return with him to the United States. The evacuees boarded a truck bound for the airport and, as he waited for any final leavers, a commune member tried to stab him. Terrified by the near miss – he appeared to have been unharmed, though the attacker had targeted his throat – Ryan left the compound.

When the truck arrived at the airport, a group of People's Temple members pulled up and started shooting at those trying to leave. Five were mortally wounded, including the congressman.

Sensing it was all over, Jim Jones performed his last act. Ordering his followers to the pavilion, he told the congregation that the US government would act fast and with brutality. He claimed that if law enforcement and other authorities arrived, the group's children and elderly members would be tortured.

The only way out, he claimed, was a "revolutionary act". Over the past two years, the compound had been receiving half-pound orders of cyanide on a monthly basis; Jones had obtained a jeweller's licence for the poison and claimed it was required to clean gold. He ordered his followers to fill kettles with the non-carbonated drink Flavor Aid, to which cyanide and Valium were added. Cups of the deadly punch were handed out to the community.

The first to consume the drink were Ruletta Paul and her one-year-old infant. Children and babies – some 300 – were killed first, their mouths filled with the poison via a syringe without a needle. Anyone who refused to drink was injected with the concoction or threatened with death by one of the armed guards. Once people had taken the drink, they were led down a walkway outside the pavilion. Children died within 5 minutes, while for adults the time was about 20 minutes. The sound of crying and screaming filled the air.

Guyanese officials arrived the following morning to a scene of utter devastation. Jim Jones, the demagogue responsible for the atrocities, lay dead from a self-inflicted gunshot wound, likely the sound that had disturbed Catherine in the night. The event received global coverage and widespread outrage, and represented an end of innocence for the United States and its sense of post-war progressive optimism. To this day, "drink the Kool-Aid" is a phrase many survivors find offensive and upsetting as it is seen to diminish the hideous repercussions of cult leadership – not to mention the fact that the drink consumed was Flavor Aid, rather than Kool-Aid. Nonetheless, it has become synonymous with the horrific events of Jonestown and the lasting and dreadful legacy of its founder.

SEAL THE DEAL

The city of Storm Lake, Iowa, has two possible stories behind its name. The first is that a local trapper (someone responsible for catching wild animals, usually to sell their fur) experienced a terrible storm on the shores of the lake at some indeterminate time in the past. The second involves a pair of lovers from rival Native American tribes, who rowed out onto the glassy surface of the lake for a tryst, but were drowned when a storm blew in.

It was here, in Storm Lake, that a woman called May Otis Blackburn was born in 1881.

Little is known about her early life and even less might be known were it not for the unusual events commencing in 1922. For some years, May Blackburn had been trying to break into the film business. This was the era of the silent movie and Blackburn founded her own production company called Starlight to make headway in the industry. It is suspected that she financed a full-length film called *The Nugget in the Rough* using funds procured in scams, one of which involved a married lumber baron (the owner of a business selling wood). For many of her movies, she would cast Ruth Wieland Rizzio, her daughter, in the leading role; nonetheless, these endeavours were not a success and before too long the money ran out.

At this point, Blackburn and Rizzio moved to Los Angeles, where they switched tack. In 1922, the pair, who often presented as sisters, began to proclaim themselves as two witnesses of the Book of Revelation. This final book of the New Testament stands out as its only apocalyptic section and it is widely agreed by scholars that its author was a Christian prophet, possibly John of Patmos. Over time Blackburn and Rizzio managed to assemble a group of followers from nearby Portland, as well as the City of Angels itself, and as word spread more members joined up.

One of Blackburn's key claims was that the angels Gabriel, who announced the birth of Jesus Christ to his mother Mary, and Michael, who is described in the Book of Revelation as doing battle with Satan, were in the process of dictating a book to herself and her daughter. The Seventh Trumpet of Gabriel soon changed to The Great Sixth Seal, and the text was purportedly filled with all the secrets of the universe, as well as a series of so-called "lost measurements" that gave the locations of hidden oil, mineral deposits and various kinds of treasure.

What was more, Blackburn claimed, the book's publication would trigger the Seventh Seal – the breakage of the final wax seal on the papyrus scroll described by John of Patmos in the Book of Revelation. At this point, she claimed, some form of apocalyptic occurrence would take place, and 11 queens would take over the world's leadership from mansions on Hollywood's Olive Hill. The Divine Order of the Royal Arms of the Great Eleven was born from this prediction, and May was its queen and high priestess. The Blackburn Cult had been born.

As the number of followers grew, so too did the group's finances. Blackburn and Rizzio asked for contributions from new members, ostensibly to support their work. These contributions could take the form of cash, valuable items and property. Rizzio, as a film actress and dancer, appeared to be the group's "honeytrap" and became adept at convincing men in particular to part with huge sums in exchange for a first glimpse of the revelatory books being dictated to the pair.

One such man was Clifford Dabney, whose uncle was an oil magnate. Dabney, who was a particularly intrigued member of the cult, "donated" $50,000 in cash and 164 acres of land in Simi Valley to Blackburn. He was informed that, if he helped to finance the book, he would be granted access to its findings three years before its publication.

It was here, on the donated land at Simi Valley, that Blackburn and her younger husband Ward Sitton Blackburn encouraged members to build cabins to wait for the Second Coming of Christ. Here they constructed a temple, including a throne set aside for Jesus himself, and gathered during the evenings for rituals including animal sacrifice and nude dancing. During the long, hot days, members were required to work in a nearby tomato-packing factory and hand over all their wages from this employment to the Blackburns.

The Simi Valley retreat might have seemed like a religious utopia from the outside but the reality was quite different. It was alleged that one member of the Blackburn Cult, Frances Turner, was placed inside a hot brick oven for two days to cure her of paralysis, resulting in her death. Four members were said to have disappeared altogether, possibly poisoned, including Rizzio's husband Samuel – who was known to be violent with her. It also appeared as though members who displayed any doubt about the self-styled "Heel of God", as May Blackburn became known, often disappeared.

Over the years that followed, the cult morphed from its original Christian belief structure into something more closely resembling paganism. Mummification of deceased members was combined with magic, nocturnal fire rituals and spirit communion.

In 1929, Clifford Dabney accused May Blackburn of fraud. The district attorney launched an investigation, finding that Blackburn had indeed defrauded not just Dabney but all her followers of some $200,000 since the cult's inception in 1922.

Once law enforcement officials began to dig into the case, they also learned of 16-year-old Willa Rhoads, a "princess" of the cult, who had died of diphtheria on 1 January 1925 and whose body was reported to have been preserved with ice, salt and spices for 14 months.

The *Los Angeles Times* reported, in a macabre twist, that during the first year of Rhoads' body's preservation her foster parents took the girl's corpse with them when they moved around with the cult and that to do so they would prop her up in the back seat of their car. "The remains," the piece ran, "were so well preserved that passers-by thought they saw a living girl."

Mrs Rhoads would go on to claim that she believed the powers of the cult might succeed in resurrecting her daughter. Once the Rhoads had lost their belief in Blackburn's power, the girl was finally buried, along with seven sacrificial dogs, under the floor of her parents' house. The dogs, it seemed, symbolized the seven notes of the angel Gabriel's trumpet.

Blackburn was charged with grand theft and, on 2 March 1930, she was convicted. On 30 November 1931, the California Supreme Court ruled that the jury had been prejudiced against Blackburn on account of reports about the suspected cult deaths. In addition, it was ruled that regulation of Blackburn's apparent power was "guarded by constitutional barriers" and went against its religious freedom principles.

Furthermore, it was claimed that "mentally healthy" people like Clifford Dabney were to be seen as responsible for their own actions when it came to association with religious orders, no matter their nature or the costs of involvement within them.

There was insufficient evidence to charge Blackburn with additional crimes and so she was freed, though the negative press of the court case and trial led to the decline of the religious movement she had created. Nonetheless, Blackburn's case was highly rare in that she was successful in avoiding jail, and, while Dabney contended that the failure to publish and print her book was fraudulent, the courts disagreed and ruled he was ultimately responsible for the donation of his own assets.

It is impossible to ascertain exactly what transpired at the Simi Valley retreat, but the media frenzy surrounding Blackburn's trial and the fascination with her personality resulted in countless column inches being dedicated to the case.

In 1936, Blackburn finally published a book containing certain sections of her proclamations; it was called *The Origin of God*. She died in Los Angeles on 17 June 1951.

A MURDEROUS AMBUSH

In 2020, 22-year-old Private Ethan Melzer from Kentucky was charged with conspiracy and attempted murder of US citizens and military-service members, and with providing material to terrorists. The acting US attorney claimed Melzer had tried "to orchestrate a murderous ambush on his own unit by unlawfully revealing its location, strength and armaments to a neo-Nazi, anarchist, white supremacist group".

That group was the Order of the Nine Angles (ONA), which was formed in the UK in the 1970s. In that decade the ONA published a series of texts designed to amass followers from all walks of life. It claimed to be a descendent of pre-Christian traditions, rites and rituals that managed to endure after the British Isles were Christianized. These traditions were reportedly passed down all the way through the Middle Ages, particularly in the Welsh Marches between England and Wales, in small groups or "temples" led by a grand master or mistress.

The Order of the Nine Angles self-identified as being of the "left-hand path": that is, a part of ceremonial black magic as opposed to "white" or benign magic. Other interpretations suggest that, while the right-hand path is associated with serving God at his side, the left advocates that godliness is found within and so refuses to subjugate itself for any deity.

In the 1960s, one of these grand mistresses merged some of the temple groups, such as Camlad, the Noctulinans and Temple of the Sun, which had likely come into being during the nineteenth-century resurgence of spiritualist and occult beliefs. It was at this point the group intended to gather more followers to its cause. The former mistress then emigrated to Australia: the group needed a new leader.

This arrived in the form of Anton Long, itself a pseudonym. Long described himself as British and claimed he'd spent his younger years visiting various countries in Africa, Asia and the Middle East. Following this, he contacted a coven – a gathering of witches – based in the eastern Fens region of England, and subsequently moved to London to practise magic associated with the divine magic of the Hermetic Order of the Golden Dawn.

When Long first met the grand mistress of the ONA, he had been involved with a Satanic group based in Manchester. Soon enough, he became the ONA's first new member in five years and was named as the heir to the grand mistress.

The group was unusual in cult terms for being a mixture of Satanism, mysticism and neo-Nazi violence. It conducted ritual ceremonies at stone circles and henges, especially around the summer solstice and the solar equinox. It is unclear exactly what the Nine Angles refers to, though one possibility is the moon, Venus, Mercury, the sun, Mars, Jupiter and Saturn, with the solar system as a whole representing the eighth angle, and the mystic the ninth. Another alternative is that the angles could refer to seven "normal" alchemical stages – calcination, dissolution, separation, conjunction, fermentation, distillation and coagulation – plus two processes related to cryptic notions of time.

RELIGIOUS CULTS

The ONA's doctrines suggest that there are set periods of time during which civilizations rise up, advance and then decline. These periods, they state, last between 1,500 and 1,700 years and are successful because a nexion, or channel, is opened that allows for a causal realm – the physical world we know – to be influenced by acausal forces such as the supernatural. According to the ONA, the current aeon marks the rise of Western civilization, but this has not been allowed to flourish successfully due to Judeo-Christian influences. As a result, it calls for a "culling" of human "scum", sacrifice and magic.

Ideally, according to the ONA, a new civilization must be brought about which combines elements of Satanism with fascism and social Darwinism. Followers are sent forth to inveigle their way into Christian churches and other organizations to wreak havoc from within. Perhaps to maintain their clandestine activities, ONA members are also required to form splinter groups across the UK and abroad. Ethics, in all forms, are considered unnecessary and irrelevant.

Neo-Nazi beliefs and the ONA have been long-time bedfellows – the latter dates its calendar from Hitler's birthday, for example – but the links were broadcast in 1998, when an anti-fascist magazine called *Searchlight* claimed that Anton Long was in fact the pseudonym of David Myatt, who was well known within British neo-Nazi circles. A founder and member of the National Socialist Movement, Myatt wrote a text called *A Practical Guide to Aryan Revolution*. This text was claimed to have been a strong influence on a young man called David Copeland.

Copeland was born in Hounslow, a suburban borough of London, in 1976. As a teenager he obtained seven GCSEs and enjoyed heavy metal music. He was reported to have feared he was gay, a fact that seems to have exacerbated his quietly brewing rage. On leaving school, he struggled to find paid employment and blamed this fact on higher levels of immigration. Soon he had turned to petty crime, drink and drugs. At the age of 21, he joined the British National Party, but left in 1998 after claiming its methods were not severe enough. He joined the National Socialist Movement instead, and in the meantime learned how to make bombs using fireworks and with alarm clocks as timers.

Over three hideous weekends in the spring of 1999, a series of home-made nail bombs were detonated across London. The first occurred in Brixton on 17 April, when a sports bag was left at the market. Concerned traders called the police, who arrived just as the bomb detonated, injuring 48 people and blowing out windows in a shower of nails.

The second bomb was left in another bag, where it was picked up by a civilian and brought to a police station, which was shut. The civilian placed the bag in the boot of his car, where it exploded, injuring 13 and damaging buildings and cars.

The third bomb was placed at the Admiral Duncan pub in the centre of the capital and detonated as the manager attempted to find out what was inside. Seventy people were injured, and four survivors underwent limb amputations. Three, sadly, were killed. Andrea Dykes, who was four months pregnant with her first child, was out with her husband Julian and her friends Nik Moore and John Light to celebrate; Light had been named as the unborn baby's godfather. Andrea, Moore and Light all died. Julian was seriously injured but survived the attack.

These terrorist attacks targeted the city's Black, Bengali and LGBT communities respectively. The dissemination of materials published by groups such as the ONA, with its large member base, is cited as a direct influence on such terrorist activities.

During the 2000s, less was heard of the ONA, which was thought to be establishing itself on social media and attempting to gather more followers. However, in 2019 a 16-year-old British boy became the youngest person in the UK to be convicted for planning a terror attack. During the trial, prosecutors argued the unnamed defendant had been influenced in part by the ONA, had studied the occult and Satanic movement's texts and had drawn a symbol for the religious group with two chilling words written beside it – "shed empathy".

LIFE AND SOLE

We've all heard of palm-reading, but what about foot-reading? By 1987, a Japanese electrician called Hogen Fukunaga had been preaching for seven years. When he first began, he was in debt, and badly – he owed some 500 million yen, just under £2.8 million in today's money. After a spiritual awakening, Fukunaga declared that he was the world's final saviour, the reincarnation of both Jesus Christ and the Buddha. While his claim may seem outlandish, his followers grew by the month, and he began to publish various ghostwritten texts that were widely disseminated as the number of his disciples grew.

In 1987, the sect gained recognition as a religious corporation, which meant it was recognized by government law. This granted Fukunaga a legitimacy that enabled still more followers to take up his cause. His group, called Ho No Hana Sanpogyo (Teaching of the Flower), was born, and Fukunaga was soon referred to as "His Holiness".

During the middle of the 1990s, Japan experienced a deep recession. Immediately following the end of World War Two, the country's economy was devastated, but bounced back quickly. As such, it underwent a period of security and stability right up until the end of the Cold War. It was during the the 1980s that the United States implemented a series of plans designed to deflate the seemingly ever-growing, unstoppable Japanese economy. One such initiative was the Semiconductor Accord in 1986, which forced leading semiconductor companies to share their intellectual properties and put in place a number of tariffs and penalties. Between 1986 and 1991 the property and stock market prices were greatly inflated, creating an economic bubble. Asset prices soared, as did money supply, credit expansion and speculation over stock prices. The Bank of Japan increased interest rates, hoping to put a damper on the real estate market, but in early 1992 the bubble burst. The Japanese were about to enter a ten-year stretch of turmoil and turbulence that came to be known as the "Lost Decade". Many young Japanese businessmen were forced to find work elsewhere. Consumption declined rapidly across the board and deflation set in.

People were desperately worried. It appeared the past 40 years had been a wonderful mirage, a dream. Now, previously bustling, booming places to live and work were winding down, businesses were going bust and any sense of security seemed laughable. As a result, many people turned to the spiritual world for help, advice and healing. Life was tough and frighteningly unpredictable: the perfect environment for cults to flourish and prosper.

Nowadays, Ho No Hana Sanpogyo is better known as the "foot-reading cult". Fukunaga claimed to be able to diagnose maladies in people by examining the soles of their feet. Initial consultations cost £750, but it was the follow-up requirements that enabled such an enormous increase in Fukunaga's personal wealth.

When new patients arrived for their appointments, they would consult on either physical or familial problems and were usually told that these would worsen unless they attended a seminar. This seminar alone would cost just under £12,500 and the alternative would be to donate six times more to the cult's coffers. At the same time, the unwitting visitors would also be urged to buy scrolls and amulets to ward off evil spirits, cure them of disease and break long-standing family "curses".

At its height, Ho No Hana Sanpogyo had amassed a staggering 30,000 members, many of them middle-aged women. The promise of familial ruin or bodily harm was often given and some followers were forced to spend many thousands on training seminars. Each member was also given specific targets with regards to recruitment and so as numbers grew so too did the money, pouring in from fresh victims who had been utterly convinced by the prognoses given either in their readings or at seminars.

Soon enough the cult's headquarters were being constructed in the city of Atami, near Mount Fuji, with a price tag of £3.3 million. This triggered a further recruitment drive, and Fukunaga encouraged his members to lie about harm that would befall potential victims, if necessary, in order to ensure new members' commitment. He even prepared a manual with which to train his followers in the art of this so-called persuasion, and claimed that during his seminars the new members would learn reason. One particular command of Fukunaga's was unequivocal: "You should use your 'wisdom' and say things, even if they may not actually be true."

The *Mainichi Shimbun* newspaper reported how one man, then in his 60s, had been in touch with Ho No Hana Sanpogyo because of fears he had contracted HIV. On examination of his feet, the man was told by Fukunaga that: "Your life is bad in the past, present and the future", before being sent on his way with the promise that he would soon be diagnosed with HIV, just as he had thought. There was, however, a possible escape. If the unwitting man handed over around £5,000 he would be granted access to a session designed to rid him of his ailments. Once this was completed, Fukunaga examined his feet once more and explained he no longer believed the man would contract HIV. Nonetheless, he was required to take a scroll home with him that day, an item that cost around £28,000.

Another man, an accountant from Tokyo, described his own experience of visiting the cult for a reading. "I took off my socks and they looked at my soles and began talking," said Kenji Sakurai. "At first I really didn't believe it 100 per cent." After 10 minutes, he was informed that his stomach was "emitting a yellow signal", an astonishing claim to Sakurai, since he'd been suffering from bellyache. The small red spot on his left foot also gave the examiners insight into the fact Sakurai would never be happily married. Since the man had arrived in Tokyo, he had been single.

Life for Sakurai had not been good of late. His eyesight was deteriorating, a relative had taken her own life and he was lonely. Here, before him, was someone promising a solution to his problems. "They said to me, 'You have great potential, but you are not fulfilling it.' One by one, he pointed out all the things that I was worrying about – I couldn't help but believe." Incredulous but hopeful, Sukurai made a payment of around £12,500 to the group.

Meanwhile, life for the once impoverished leader was going very well indeed. He wore expensive suits and custom Italian shoes. His wife often spent between £5,000 and £6,000 a month on shopping alone.

At the height of his power, Fukunaga had obtained the equivalent in yen of £620 million from his supporters, some of which was spent paying for access to influential public figures like Pope John Paul II, Bill Clinton, Margaret Thatcher, Mother Teresa and the Soviet president Mikhail Gorbachev. Indeed, at one fundraising dinner in 1996, a distant relative of Mahatma Gandhi paid for his ticket and for Fukunaga's using a £270,000 contribution fee. During the event, the two men presented President Clinton with the Gandhi Peace Award.

Over time, suspicions grew. Family members of those involved in the cult began to suggest that Fukunaga was misappropriating the funds paid by their relatives. The man who had believed he would contract HIV filed a lawsuit with Shizuoka District Court for reparations of £41,000. The Kyodo News Service subsequently ran a piece explaining that four members of Ho No Hana Sanpogyo had in fact died during their training. The report also stated that members of the group were not allowed to sleep during the training session, which could last four or five days, and that, when their physical and mental fatigue were at their worst, the group forcibly persuaded them to pay a few more million yen to buy articles such as a hanging scroll.

The family of one man was planning to file a lawsuit against the cult because their relative had fallen from the window of a second-floor bathroom during a five-day training session. When investigated, it transpired the local Fuji fire service had received 12 similar calls over the past five years alone. Falling from windows was, surely, not as common as this. Over time, 1,200 suits were filed against the cult.

In 1999, after a series of police raids at the group's facilities, Fukanaga was arrested and charged with multiple counts of fraud. In January 2000, he resigned as leader of Ho No Hana Sanpogyo. In December of that year, Tokyo District Court ruled that the actions of the group went well beyond what could be socially justified by demanding that its followers part with large sums of money. The cult was found guilty of fortune-telling fraud and practising medicine without a licence. Fukanaga, along with 15 other senior members of the cult, was sentenced to 12 years in prison. The cult as a whole was ordered to pay almost £830,000 to the 16 people they had falsely claimed would develop cancer unless they joined Ho No Hana Sanpogyo.

The once untouchable leader attempted to claim that the legal system was breaching his right to freedom of religion, but the judge disagreed, stating the episode was nothing but fraud.

A new leadership was announced in the aftermath of Fukunaga's resignation, and the latter said it would "continue to be run based on *tensei* (the voice of heaven)" – a voice, he claimed, his followers believed only he himself could hear.

The case represented a particular challenge to police, it seems, due to the reluctance of Japanese law enforcement officials to interfere with religious groups – especially ones that had been recognized as corporations. It was only after the release from prison of a senior member of another cult, Aum Shinrikyo (see page 106), that police started to feel more confident in questioning the methods and practices of religious sects.

A FIERY BAPTISM

By the late eighteenth century, Russia was the largest country in the world, spanning many thousands of miles from the Black Sea to the Bering Strait. Travelling from one side to the other by train took around ten days – this vast swathe of land was challenging to govern, but, despite its size, it was for the most part extremely poor. The deeply engrained, entrenched hierarchical system in Russia at the time allowed landowning noblemen to operate with complete fiscal controls over serfs who usually had none, and the middle class was too small to provide any real resistance.

As a result, farmers and peasants from all over the country, terrified by the prospect of starvation, emigrated to the United States. Of course, in the early twentieth century the Russian Revolution would result in the murder of Tsar Nicholas II, his wife and children at the hands of the Bolsheviks, the group that would become the Communist Party and the rulers of the Soviet Union. In the century before the revolution, the country was struggling, while the official Russian Orthodox Church was beginning to be seen as inflexible, bureaucratic and outdated. Those looking for a new means of expressing their faith were about to find one.

In the late eighteenth century, a new religious movement emerged in Russia, called the Skoptsy. The Russian population then was growing at an exponential rate but remained largely rural. It was a time of deprivation, discontent and marginalization – the perfect conditions for a new sect to take root.

Virtually all Christian beliefs discourage sex before marriage. Lust, one of the seven deadly sins, was considered to be a mortal social ill, and it was this that the Skoptsy clan adopted as its focal point. The Skoptsy stemmed from Spiritual Christianity, a branch of Protestantism (brought over from Europe by missionaries) and non-Eastern Orthodox faith tribes that emerged within the Russian Empire.

Skoptsky is a derivation of *oskopit*, an obsolete Russian word meaning "to castrate". The group's members, however, preferred to call themselves other, less brutal names, such as God's Lambs, or White Doves.

Alarming reports soon began to circulate about the practices of the Skoptsy, which advocated so strongly against lust in any form that it castrated its male followers and performed mastectomies on its female ones. This was known as "fiery baptism". There were two primary methods of castration, called the "lesser" and "greater" seals. For men, the former involved the removal of the testicles, while the latter removed both the penis and testicles using a red-hot iron. The scrotum was also twisted to destroy the seminal vesicles. For women, the castration involved removal of the nipples, the whole breasts, the labia minora and the clitoris. None of these procedures were ever performed with anaesthetic, and they were generally performed by elders who would chant "Christ is risen!" while conducting their grisly rite.

Self-castration has not only been observed by those practising the Skoptic faith; the ancient Christian theologian Origen was said to have performed the same act of self-mutilation.

Christians had taken this tiding from a verse in the Gospel of Matthew: "There are castrates who were castrated by others and there are castrates who castrated themselves for the Kingdom of God." Sex, it was believed, was sin no matter the context and the only way to guard against it was to remove the believed source of the sex drive.

The Skoptsky believed that removal of the sex organs, which they saw as the mark of Cain, would "perfect" the body and remove original sin, itself brought about by the first intercourse between Adam and Eve. The group maintained that Jesus had advocated for the practice and had been a eunuch himself, along with his apostles and the early saints of Christianity.

Although it took time to gather momentum, the movement was first identified in the 1760s as a splinter group of another sect called the Khlysts, which itself had split from the Russian Orthodox Church. Three fathers of the Khlysts were said to have castrated themselves and 30 others, one of whom was Kondratiy Ivanovich Selivanov, who started his own religious cult in the village of Sosnovka, over 250 miles south-east of Moscow.

Selivanov amassed followers quickly, and in 1772 246 followers of the new movement were put on trial, with the leader convicted of having persuaded a number of peasants to castrate themselves. The so-called "Son of God" and "Redeemer" managed to escape after his sentence but was caught three years later and exiled to Siberia.

Such was the power of Selivanov's personality that despite the lack of transportation options available to them his loyal followers were able to track him down, free him and help him move back to Moscow. The story became ever more bizarre when, in 1797, he relocated to St Petersburg, where he obtained an audience with Tsar Paul I and claimed to be his assassinated father Peter III: "I am not the father of sin," he told the tsar. "Accept my act and I will recognize you as my son." Paul I had him sent to a madhouse in response.

Five years passed until his release, whereupon Selivanov remained in St Petersburg at the house of a follower. Worshippers continued to flock to his cause, particularly when he announced himself not only as Peter III, the former tsar, but also as the returned figure of Jesus Christ. His key tenet was that salvation was achievable only through castration, and several prominent city figures and aristocrats were known to have joined the cause. In 1804, one such aristocrat, Alexei Yelensky, sent a proposal to the Russian emperor requesting that the country be given over to the power of the Skoptsy.

The nephews of St Petersburg's governor general were among these new members, as were guards and sailors. In frustration and fear, the governor asked that something be done about Selivanov, who was arrested in the summer of 1820 and sent to Evfimiev monastery, in a town called Suzdal to the northeast of Moscow, where he remained for the next 12 years until his death.

He was never released, but his disciples were permitted to visit him at the monastery, and they were able to access his "teachings" posthumously through the writings he left behind.

The tsar's police service vehemently hoped that Selivanov's death would mark an end to the actions of this gruesome sect, but his followers continued to flourish across the country's major cities and even in Bucharest and Iași in Romania. In the meantime, various measures were implemented to try to dissuade the Skoptsy from proliferating: male members, if caught and convicted, were dressed in women's clothes and fools' caps and forced to parade through the streets. Some were deported. Many emigrated, often to Romania.

In 1866, the Skoptsy boasted some 5,444 members, three quarters of whom were men. Its adherents hailed both from provincial, illiterate, impoverished areas of the country and from the more upper-class merchant houses in St Petersburg.

Despite the death of their erstwhile leader, the popularity of the Skoptsy continued apace and, during the second half of the nineteenth century, they were well known throughout Russia. The sect even made it into the novels of Fyodor Dostoevsky, who wrote in *The Idiot* that "The skopets who holds the shop generally lodges upstairs."

As time went on, the group amassed a great deal of wealth and used some of these funds to bring about more conversions, enable shelter for orphans and provide money to the poor. If authorities had wanted to clamp down on the group's activities, it would have been hard-pressed to do so – it was often easier to ignore societal issues such as these, particularly with such large, unwieldy territories to manage. If a branch of the Skoptsky was outcast or deemed unpalatable in some way, it could easily move to another area without detection or much consequence.

By the early twentieth century, the sect was at the height of its powers. Reports vary as to exact numbers, but the highest estimate suggests 1 million members; certainly there were hundreds of thousands. It was only as the Soviet Union clamped down on the group, expanded its collectivist policies, arrested members and put the sect on a highly publicized trial that membership began to dwindle. Today, it is largely believed that the sect has faded into obsolescence, a likelihood given further credence by the fact that existing members were unable to bear children and thereby pass on the Skoptsy doctrines.

THE SUM OF SQUARES

"In a right-angled triangle, the square of the hypotenuse side is equal to the sum of squares of the other two sides." If we cast our collective mind back to maths lessons, we might remember these words as Pythagoras' theorem. However, the Greek mathematician and philosopher was involved in more than geometry: in fact, he also founded a school of thought that became an ancient cult.

Little is known of Pythagoras' early life but he was most likely born on the island of Samos, on the eastern side of the Aegean Sea. The poet Heraclitus was born nearby and is known to have mocked Pythagoras, inadvertently giving another clue as to his ancestry: "Pythagoras, son of Mnesarchus, practiced inquiry more than any other man, and selecting from these writings he manufactured a wisdom for himself – much learning, artful knavery."

Historical sources indicate Mnesarchus, Pythagoras' father, was a gem-maker from Tyre, while his mother was Pythais, a native of Samos. Legend suggests the pair met when Mnesarchus brought corn to the island during a famine and was granted citizenship as a result. The couple's son was born in 570 BCE. Although the birth order is unclear, Pythagoras had at least two brothers and perhaps three.

Pythagoras travelled more in his early life than the average boy at the time. Often accompanying his father, the youngster visited Tyre, where he was taught by various learned men, and also visited Italy. He learned to play the lyre and recite the poetry of Homer, even learning it off by heart. He was principally taught by three philosophers, one of whom was called Pherecydes, and developed a keen interest in mathematics, astronomy, geometry and cosmology. In 535 BCE he travelled to Egypt, likely with a letter of recommendation from Polycrates, the self-appointed tyrant who governed Samos. There he is said to have visited the temples, conversed with priests and eventually himself been accepted into the priesthood.

Having adopted many of these practices and beliefs of the Egyptian priests, his next stop was Crotone in southern Italy, where in around 530 BCE Pythagoras founded a school. Its students – both men and women – lived a communal and deeply spiritual life, isolated from modern society and deeply committed to the notion of abstaining from sensual or earthly pleasures in order to achieve enlightenment. Sexual relations were banned in summer but encouraged in winter; bread could not be broken with bare hands and fires couldn't be stirred with iron.

Followers had no possessions, were strict vegetarians and were banned from wearing clothes made from the skins of animals. Beans were also banned as Pythagoras declared they contained the souls of the dead; moreover, flatulence signified part of the soul being lost. Followers were required, at all times, to put their right shoe on before the left. When a new member joined, they were committed to a vow of silence lasting five years.

The society's inner circle were known as *mathematikoi*, and they were taught by Pythagoras himself. The key rules governing the school were founded on the ideas that reality was mathematical in nature, that philosophy could purify the soul (which itself could become one with the divine) and that certain symbols possessed a mystical significance. Additionally, the "brothers of the order" were required to observe strict loyalty and secrecy. It was, in every modern sense of the word, a religious and philosophical cult. Followers were encouraged to "be like your Master".

The school is known as the home of major contributions to the study of mathematics, its principles and concepts. Aristotle wrote that "The Pythagorean... having been brought up in the study of mathematics, thought that things are numbers... and that the whole cosmos is a scale and a number." Pythagoras believed that numbers had personalities – masculine, feminine, perfect, incomplete, beautiful or ugly – and his political and religious teachings would go on to influence the likes of Plato and Aristotle himself.

It was these more unusual, spiritual forays into the world of mathematical study that gained Pythagoras a reputation beyond the academic. His deep conviction that the mysteries of the universe could be understood through numerical formulae meant his image encompassed both teacher and spiritual leader. This was enhanced through the lifestyle adopted by the commune he had created, the strict daily rules that governed his students and their belief in metempsychosis, or reincarnation.

The Pythagorean school of thought also believed in "universal music" and understood the movement of the solar system to be a form of harmony. They advocated for transmigration of the soul: in other words, that human souls could exist in the bodies of animals, which was the reason for their vegetarian diet. On one occasion, Pythagoras witnessed a man beating a dog and intervened because he could tell, from the sound of the barking, that the dog was in fact an old friend of his – his soul had moved into the animal. When it came to his own previous lives, the cult leader was able to pinpoint four iterations: as the son of Hermes, a fisherman, a courtesan and a soldier in the Trojan War.

Pythagoras' followers certainly believed their leader to be, if not a god, then a demigod, possessed of supernatural powers and ancient, powerful wisdom. He was addressed as "the divine" and rumours spread that he was the son of Apollo or Hermes. It seems the man did little to dispel such notions and songs of praise were written in his honour. His most devout followers claimed he could tame eagles and bears, control any animal simply by addressing it and appear in two places at once. Aristotle went on to write of Pythagoras' supposed "golden thigh", on view for all to see at one iteration of the Olympic Games.

Increasingly, followers came to regard the man as having been sent from heaven to show them the importance of worshipping numbers. Each digit represented a different virtue, with four being justice and five being marriage, for example. The number ten was the most blessed of all, being a pyramid of four, three, two and one dots, a symbol known as a tetractys.

As word spread about Pythagoras and his teachings, other Pythagorean communes emerged along the southern coast of Italy. Those who did not approve of the man or his methods became increasingly enraged. It is likely that his followers attempted to disseminate their world view beyond the commune and the locals of Crotone reacted negatively. Who were these strange people to tell them how to dress or what to eat? Over time, the Pythagoreans fell victim to sustained attacks of persecution, and many were killed.

In 480 BCE, locals reportedly started a fire at the Pythagorean meeting ground, though it is unclear whether the man himself died in the attack. Legend has it that some followers lay down in the flames to allow him to walk over them and escape, leading to his guilt-induced suicide afterwards. In another version of events, he managed to leave the building but ran straight into a field of beans and, being unable to cross it due to his beliefs, remained at its edge until the locals bore down upon him. Both versions may be true in part or entirely false. In another retelling of the leader's demise, followers threw him into the sea after the discovery of the famous theorem, convinced it would disrupt their belief systems and the world order they had spent years studying.

Scholars have no access to his original writings, as none survived. For some years after his death, the Cult of Pythagoras continued to regroup, before slowly dissipating. Without their charismatic, highly intelligent leader, his followers were unable to sustain the world view they had cultivated over so many years.

V-DAY

After Japan's surrender at the end of World War Two in 1945, the Korean peninsula was freed from its control and the 38th parallel was established as the border between the Democratic People's Republic of Korea to the north and the Republic of Korea to the south. The principle of the 38th parallel was to divide Korea into two occupation zones, with the United States occupying the south, and the Soviet Union holding the north. The arrangement was to be temporary, but that would soon change.

On Thursday 25 June 1950, South Korea was invaded by the Korean People's Army from the north, a formidable force of some 75,000 soldiers. At its heart, the conflict revolved around communism, and it was the first military event of the Cold War, which spanned decades and finally came to an end in 1991. Over the next three years, between 2 and 4 million people lost their lives, 70 per cent of them civilians. Although the fighting officially ended in 1953, it wasn't until December 2021 that both North and South Korea, as well as the United States and China, agreed that the war was formally over.

After the outbreak of war, the United Nations Security Council deemed that North Korea was the aggressor and gave permission for armed intervention to aid South Korea.

The National Christian Council in South Korea asked for help from the United States, and soon enough churches across Western nations called for UN support.

However, Eastern European churches disagreed and felt that UN intervention amounted to attempts to block Asian people's freedom. Since these Christian churches were seen to be adopting pro-American outlooks, North Korea's regime classified Christianity as an unpatriotic religion. This move was to have serious, long-term consequences for people of that faith within both North and South Korea, long after the civil war was ostensibly over.

Over the next three years, the North Korean military was ordered to "eliminate reactionary forces" and killed 1,026 Christians and 119 Catholics as it retreated from South Korea. The massacres were concentrated in, but not limited to, the central province of South Chungcheong and south-western province of Jeolla. It was in the latter region that 167 elders and members of a Protestant church were burned to death in one shocking attack at Jeongeup. It was against this anti-Christian backdrop that the seeds of a new and bizarre cult were first planted.

When the war broke out, Cho Hee-Seung was 21 years old. He was born in Gimpo, in the Gyeonggi province of South Korea. Little is known about exactly how his incarceration came about during the war at the hands of the Red Army but what is certain is the motive for his imprisonment: his Christianity. He was interned at a concentration camp during the first month of the conflict as an anti-communist prisoner of war and was not released until 1953. Upon his release he joined the South Korean army and became a second lieutenant.

At this point, Cho continued to explore his faith in both the Methodist and Presbyterian denominations, attending services at different churches. Cho's fascination stemmed in part from his reading of the Bible, which claimed Christians would enjoy resurrection and enter the kingdom of heaven after the death of their earthly bodies. Soon enough, he sought out Park Tae-Seon, the man responsible for founding the new religious movement, Olive Tree. During the 1970s, a staggering 1.5 million followers joined the cause; Cho had joined earlier, serving as a missionary for the Olive Tree movement throughout the 1960s and into the next decade, and founding churches dedicated to the group across South Korea.

In 1980, Cho was on a retreat at one of the Olive Tree "Faith Villages" around 16 miles away from South Korea's capital, Seoul. It was here, in a "secret chamber", that Cho was recognized by a shaman as "the Victor Christ" and "God incarnated", the last of a sequence of so-called angels that included Abraham, Isaac, Jacob and Olive Tree seniors, culminating with Cho himself.

Cho, amazed and awestruck, decided to leave Olive Tree and create his own movement, SeungNiJeDan (the Victory Altar). According to Cho, Jesus was a false prophet and the true Holy Trinity was comprised of God, Adam and Eve, who were all gods but limited in their power, unlike the traditional image of God as the omnipotent Father.

Cho proclaimed that Satan invaded the Garden of Eden 6,000 years ago, took Adam and Eve as his prisoners and made them mortal, though their children and descendants through the ages would possess a small portion of the divinity they had once enjoyed. In Cho's doctrines, Satan himself was the forbidden fruit, taking the place of the fabled apple. Since

God alone had not been captured by Satan, he was required to undergo a journey to restore humankind's immortality. A part of this crusade involved the creation of the aforementioned divine prophets, who were sent out into the world to spread the Gospel.

The Battle of Armageddon described in the Bible, as well as the resurrection of Christ, did not, according to Cho, take place in the Middle East but in 1980 inside the secret chamber at the Olive Tree headquarters. It was here, Cho claimed, that he conquered the blood of Satan, his own ego, and morphed into the Victor Christ. God, now, was able at last to defeat Satan and return to Earth through Cho. According to the Victory Altar, Jesus of Nazareth had been born to Mary, but his father was not Joseph: it had been Pantera, a Roman soldier. Cho proclaimed that Jesus went on to marry Mary Magdalene, a departure from scriptures that was explored two decades later in Dan Brown's bestselling novel *The Da Vinci Code*.

Cho established his new group's headquarters in Bucheon, the same city that had played host to the initial retreat at Olive Tree. Within just a few years, Victory Altar boasted 400,000 followers. In 1984, nine Victory Altars had been established across the country, while the cult was formed in both Japan and the United States in 1986. The majority of Cho's disciples were native to South Korea but branches increasingly spread to Australia, New Zealand and the United Kingdom. By August 1991, the facility at Bucheon was complete and the group's new worship services were unveiled.

Services at the facility were offered five times a day and consisted of songs and sermons led by Cho. Throughout the year, feasts celebrated "Victory Day", when Cho was proclaimed Victor Christ, and Christmas Day became Messiah

Day, which gave thanks for the prophecies and doctrines of other religions but concluded they were brought about through Cho himself. Christmas was moved to 12 August, Cho's own birthday. Alongside the feasts and worship, however, cult members experienced forced labour, exploitation and worse abuses should they attempt to leave or disagree with Cho's belief systems.

All the while, both the Korean anti-cult movement and more traditional Christian churches condemned Cho's practices as heretical. The South Korean president, Kim Young-sam, was himself a Presbyterian Christian and many of those most vehemently opposed to Cho were connected to the politician. It is thought that this affiliation proved instrumental in the hostile media landscape that became increasingly opposed to Cho and Victory Altar. The notion that Jesus Christ had been the "son of Satan", and the suggestion that he had married Mary Magdalene in particular, brought about a bitter conflict between traditional Christian theism and Cho's doctrines.

One of Cho's key tenets was his own immortality, which manifested through Hidden Manna or Holy Dew, secreted from his body – and even portraits bearing his likeness, when he was not physically present. These signs took the form of smoke, blood, fog and fire, and were said to act as a form of nourishment to his followers. Cho also promised through five key covenants that communism would be destroyed around the world, typhoons would cease their destructive patterns over South Korea, harvests would be plentiful and the rainy season would end.

There would, Cho claimed, never again be war in Korea and both sides of the peninsula would be united. Such promises would have had broad appeal to followers of the Victory Altar, particularly after the decades of post-war Christian persecution in North Korea. Assurances that the country – so devastated by the conflict in the 1950s – would become prosperous and enjoy periods of peace, stability and economic growth were clearly welcome as forward-looking notions, whether they were grounded in truth or not.

In early January 1994, Cho was arrested and remanded in prison to await trial for the exploitation of workers at his headquarters, fraud charges and for holding members against their will. He was accused, too, of having ordered the deaths of certain anti-cultists and ex-members of the Victory Altar, whose deaths had occurred over the previous four years. He was ultimately found not guilty of this latter charge, but in 1996 was convicted on the fraud counts and sentenced to jail. After six years he was released on parole.

In 2003, reports began to circulate that former members of the group had indeed been secretly buried at its headquarters. When police investigated, 15 bodies were found at the Bucheon organization, and Cho was re-arrested after prosecutors claimed the murderers of Victory Altar's ex-members had identified him as the initiator behind the killings. At this point, the once powerful leader was given the death sentence and a date was set for his execution. An appeal, however, found him not guilty; prosecutors in turn appealed this verdict. Before a final verdict could be reached, though, Cho died, on 19 June 2004.

Despite their shock at his death, this event did not represent a problem to his followers, since Cho was believed to be immortal. They declared that his previous corporeal form might have passed over, but that he had surely assumed a new body. A new president assumed the administrative responsibilities of cult leader but Cho continued to lead his congregations via video screens in pre-recorded films, and was seen long after 2004 singing, preaching and asking his followers questions in the eerie clips.

Over time, however, the deaths of early members and the difficulty in establishing their previously accepted immortality led to declining adherence to the Victory Altar. It is thought some 40 Victory Altars remain today in South Korea, with a few also surviving in Japan. Most interestingly, it is believed that smaller congregations still meet privately in the United States, Australia, New Zealand and the United Kingdom. In 2017, Victory Altar was believed to have around 100,000 members.

During the Covid-19 pandemic, the city of Bucheon announced that 53 cases of coronavirus had been identified in a congregation of nearly 300 of the Victory Altar church. Part of the reason the virus had spread so quickly, it seemed, was that church members had been living together, in sex-segregated dormitories. Despite the waning numbers of this once enormous membership, there are clearly still very strong pockets of belief dedicated to the man who styled himself as Victor Christ.

FUNDAMENTALLY EVIL

In 1890, the state of Utah outlawed the practice of polygamy. It had been given a clear ultimatum by Washington, DC and officials had been informed that the only way to achieve statehood and effectively join the unified country from a legal, federal and economic perspective was to change its stance on multiple marriages. For the previous four decades, Congress had refused Utah's petitions to join on exactly these grounds.

The president of Utah's dominant Church of Jesus Christ of Latter-day Saints, Wilford Woodruff, denied that his church taught polygamy but nonetheless agreed to follow the federal law. In 1896, Utah was officially made a state.

For many members of the Church, this break with tradition was hard to stomach. While certain congregants adopted the new rules, others refused. Some were excommunicated and others broke off from the umbrella Church voluntarily to form their own branch.

Since polygamy was now forbidden in Utah, the new sect moved to the borderlands of north-western Arizona, where they continued to practise polygamy. In the towns of Hildale and Colorado City, the first Fundamentalist Church of Jesus Christ of Latter-Day Saints (FLDS) colonies were founded in 1902. These remote areas were the perfect locations as they gave the groups relative privacy from other towns and villages and allowed the members to avoid state legislation or law enforcement by crossing the border as and when required.

The FLDS is the largest of the Latter Day Saint movements. It is called "Fundamentalist" because it holds to Mormonism's founding beliefs, those taught by the religion's founders, Brigham Young and Joseph Smith. Other fundamental Mormon doctrines relate, for example, to the idea of a "United Order", wherein communities were established that aimed to abolish social hierarchies and income discrepancies, eradicate poverty and create an egalitarian communal utopia.

The Mormon group's original founding members called themselves the Council of Friends. The community in its earliest forms appears to have garnered little controversy, perhaps because law enforcement officials rarely approached the new communities or because polygamy was still widely viewed as socially acceptable in the immediate aftermath of its outlawing.

For the group's first followers, scripture was a mixture of the King James Bible, the Book of Mormon, the Pearl of Great Price and the Doctrine and Covenants. Polygamy was not just a preference but a requirement, since they believed a man could only enter heaven if he had taken at least three wives during the course of his life. Members were told that having more wives meant having more children, thus leading them closer to heaven. According to the Mormon fundamentalists, the Gospels were clear that Jesus Christ had ordained the practice of plural marriage.

The Council of Friends later changed its name to the more commonly known Fundamentalist Church of Jesus Christ of Latter-Day Saints. Leroy S. Johnson was proclaimed the group's leader in 1949 following the death of its former head and three years later the sect was officially separated from the Latter-day Saints Church.

The FLDS forbade the inclusion of any Black members and instigated a dress code for female followers. Women were forbidden to wear either trousers or make-up and instead were required to wear long dresses and keep their hair long and styled to be able to wash the feet of Jesus when he came to Earth once more.

The Fundamentalists first made headlines in the summer of 1953 when police raided the group's compound in Short Creek, Arizona, and arrested 263 children and around 150 adults. Since many of the children were separated from their parents, the state's actions were regarded in a dim light by many both within and outside the branch.

Over the following decades, many subgroups and splinter segments formed in the wake of the Fundamentalists: these offshoots included the Church of the Lamb of God and the Church of the New Covenant in Christ.

By 1986, the Fundamentalists were led by Rulon Jeffs, whose parents had been polygamists. He is believed to have coined the phrase "keep sweet, pray and obey", a way of explaining to the women in the group the importance of total obedience to their male counterparts. When men married for the second or even third time, their new partners and any subsequent children often lived downstairs within the family home, while first wives and the children from that union lived upstairs – a far cry from the egalitarian utopia first espoused.

On Rulon Jeffs' death in 2002, the mantle was passed to his son, Warren. The Fundamentalists now had around 10,000 followers in the core Arizona–Utah borderland, but there were other groups located in Mexico and in British Columbia in Canada.

By the time of his death, Rulon Jeffs had 75 wives and 65 children. Once he had been proclaimed leader, Warren Jeffs was seen as solely responsible for communicating God's messages to the Fundamentalists. His first action was to marry his father's wives, and soon enough he instructed members to remove their children from school.

Warren Jeffs' leadership was far more dramatic and draconian than that of his father and soon enough followers were banned from any organized sports, meeting for social events, going on holiday, reading books or newspapers, going camping or fishing, or owning dogs or televisions. "If you're questioning me," one former member recalled being told, "you're questioning God."

One of the most significant issues caused by the group's focus on polygamy was the ostracization of young male members. Many within this demographic were excluded from the Fundamentalists, often while only teenagers, because they were seen as representing competition with the older males of the group. These "Lost Boys" were encouraged to find a life elsewhere and often found themselves wandering the desert alone without food, water or money.

Life at the commune was just as grim for the women, who were assigned husbands when they came of age and sometimes before. These women could then be taken by Warren Jeffs as their own wife or given to another man entirely in a practice called "placing". Escape, should anybody want to leave, was difficult. The first communes were extremely remote and departure would mean almost certain death. The arid, desolate deserts were hard to navigate and survive even for experts, and still more so for people with limited experience of the world outside their commune.

According to Jeffs, too, fraud was a noble act and one that all members should commit where possible. "Bleeding the beast" was the practice of claiming huge sums in welfare benefits, a ruse made possible because "plural wives" were not legally married to their husbands in the eyes of the government. Therefore, they could apply for and receive aid from the federal coffers – money that was always passed straight on to their husbands or to Jeffs himself. In order to evade any scrutiny, new babies' birth certificates were doctored so the identity of their true father was withheld. Often, entirely fictitious names were chosen to divert attention from the polygamy being practised.

By 2003 the Fundamentalists were living on a Texan ranch called Yearning For Zion (YFZ) in Eldorado. Here a grand white temple was constructed, along with homes for commune members; Jeffs himself had a house of 2,700 square metres. In 2004, Jeffs expelled 20 men from the Short Creek community and "redistributed" their wives and their children to other male members.

Generally, polygamy is rarely prosecuted in the United States. Evidence can be hard to prove beyond doubt and law enforcement and social services are also unwilling to break up families. Were it not for the allegations emerging from the Texan ranch, which were often anonymous, life might have continued for the Fundamentalists much as it had done before. However, in 2006 Warren Jeffs was placed on the FBI's Ten Most Wanted list for charges of arranging marriages between men and underage girls. The reward for his capture stood at $60,000. He was arrested during a traffic stop in Las Vegas on 28 August 2006 and taken into custody. Inside the car, police discovered multiple laptops, credit cards, disguises, huge amounts of cash and audio tapes that, when played, were found to be recordings of Jeffs having sex with underage girls at the Texan ranch.

In 2007, Jeffs was found guilty of rape and was sentenced to ten years, imprisonment in Utah. This sentence was later overturned due to an error in the instruction of the jury. In the meantime, police in Texas raided the YFZ ranch and took custody of over 400 children living there; many were later returned to the community because of insufficient evidence of abuse. However, 11 adults who were arrested were charged and convicted for crimes ranging from sexual assault of a child to bigamy and conducting unlawful weddings.

Jeffs was sent to Texas for a new trial, where he was found guilty again of sex with minors. For this crime he received life plus 20 years, and he remains in prison in Texas to this day. He continues to disseminate his teachings even from prison, however, and published a book in 2012 called *Jesus Christ Message to All Nations*. In the work, Jeffs claimed that his release alone could prevent the apocalypse from descending on Earth.

In the Colorado City and Hildare communities, subsequent investigations found the world's highest proportion of what has been described as "Polygamist Down's Syndrome", a direct consequence of marriages between cousins. This had resulted in gene mutations, causing birth defects, with many children born with microcephaly (where the head is far smaller than expected) and suffering from weak muscles, epileptic seizures and learning difficulties.

The cult gradually reduced in the years that followed and public meetings were no longer held. Some women left the commune voluntarily, while others remained to champion Jeffs' innocence and pray for his release. Perhaps knowing that leadership of the cult would likely lead to arrest, no new leaders have been appointed.

THE SEX GURU

India, 1931. The British government relocated the country's capital from the eastern city of Calcutta to Delhi, in the north, in a bid designed to make administration and management easier. The 62-year-old Mohandas Gandhi had recently been released from prison for what the British government deemed "political crimes". His landmark work *Hind Swaraj*, published over 20 years before, had claimed that the Indian population had co-operated with its own subjugation by the British, and the only way of achieving independence from the empire was to end this co-operation.

In 1930, he had written and sent a letter to the viceroy of India, Lord Irwin, in which he described British rule in his country as a "curse" that had "impoverished the dumb millions"; he explained that Irwin's salary alone amounted to more than 5,000 times India's average income.

It was a turbulent time for the country and one of great social, political and economic change. Chandra Mohan Jain was born into this climate of uncertainty and rebellion and grew up in the central Madhya Pradesh. He lived with his maternal grandparents until he was eight years old and he would later describe the considerable freedom and lack of rules afforded him by his grandmother, which in turn engendered an inquiring mind, a certain comfort with rebellion and the development of socialist principles.

Jain, or Rajneesh as he was known, was an equal parts intelligent and rebellious child. He read widely and was regarded as an excellent debater. He became interested in religion from a young age but dismissed the more traditional expressions of his Jain faith in favour of yoga, meditation, fasting and a growing interest in the occult. His school would later attempt to expel him for reading Karl Marx and Friedrich Engels, which labelled him, in his teachers' eyes, a communist. Nonetheless, Rajneesh formed a small group of friends concerned with discussions of religion and its shortcomings and who shared communist principles. He would later become fascinated further by anarchism, revolution and personal freedom.

Rajneesh studied philosophy at the University of Jabalpur and graduated in 1955. He began teaching at the same university two years later. At the age of 21, however, he experienced an apparent moment of epiphany, a spiritual awakening that prompted him to resign his post and commit to a life of preaching against traditional, mainstream religions, as well as the political creeds espoused by Gandhi and his followers. By 1970, Rajneesh was in Mumbai, quickly gathering followers, who became known as "neo-sannyasins", to his cause.

This new movement described itself as being world-centric, its focus being awareness of energy, form and experience, and a rejection of authoritarianism, formalization or its own recognized legitimacy as a "religion". All religious experiences were inextricably linked to the broader definition of a spiritual life, and were deeply personal, individual and separate from and in opposition to the single belief structure of organized religions. Rajneesh was now a teacher of meditation, a guru.

He encouraged his new followers to reject the earthly world and turn instead to asceticism, the practice of denying oneself physical or mental desires in favour of a higher truth achieved through spiritual, meditative means. They would live in the world, but without attachment to it.

In 1974, Rajneesh established an ashram (a sacred place) in Poona, now Pune, on the 21st anniversary of his original spiritual epiphany. The headquarters were located in Koregaon Park and were purchased with funds from a Greek shipping heiress. Catherine Venizelos, who changed her name to Ma Yoga Mukta, had been on a visit to India, where she met Rajneesh and joined his movement. Rajneesh would later describe Mukta as a miracle. Between 1974 and 1981 Rajneesh preached his teachings at the ashram, which had two houses and over 24,000 square metres of land. Here his sermons were recorded both aurally and on to film. "I have been working hard," he stated, "to abandon everything that is outer, so that only the inner remains for you to explore." As time went on, so too did Rajneesh's use of drugs, namely Valium and nitrous oxide, which were reportedly to manage the pain of different health issues.

His audience grew, and the number of Western devotees such as Ma Yoga Mukta increased exponentially. In addition to gaining spiritual succour, devotees also produced clothes, jewellery, pottery and organic make-up at the facility's dedicated craft centre and were involved with theatre and musical productions. Whole families often moved to the ashram, some from previously very ordinary, middle-class lives in the United Kingdom and the United States. Children spent their days roaming freely, singing songs with their teachers – they did not learn to read, write or do arithmetic – and slept in dormitories in octagonal bamboo structures away from their parents.

Soon enough, therapists arrived from the Human Potential Movement, which had begun to take root in multiple countries in the 1960s, and which advocated for the untapped happiness and fulfilment of every human being. The movement's central tenet was espoused that humankind as a whole possesses an immense and often unrealized potential.

When these therapists arrived, Rajneesh's organization turned also to meditative therapy groups, which members paid handsomely to attend.

Each day began at 6 a.m. with a dynamic meditation session, followed by an hour lecture that alternated between Hindi and English in the "Buddha Hall". Members consulted Rajneesh personally about which therapies to join throughout the day; these included experimental bouts of physical aggression between usually naked participants, often involving pillows but sometimes with their fists. One therapist, Richard Price, later recalled being locked in a room for 8 hours alongside other members wielding wooden sticks and weapons; he left the ashram with a broken arm.

Drug-fuelled orgies – sometimes in padded rooms, presumably for the participants' own physical safety – were frequent occurrences, with one ex-member, who grew up at the ashram, reporting: "You could hear people having orgasmic sex all the time. All night, like mating baboons, gibbons."

The cult's unrestrained and free attitude towards sex and sexuality soon became one of its most infamous attributes. One of the main issues with this was that men outnumbered women at the ashram five to one, and ex-members later recounted how any single female members would have to "make themselves available" to single men in a form of "new surrender". Men were permitted to approach any woman they chose and were even placed on waiting lists for sexual encounters with them. When a German actress called Eva Renzi refused to sleep with a man who desired her, a group of followers punched and kicked her, ripping her clothes off. Disturbingly, Rajneesh often chose the cult's most beautiful women to act as "energy mediums" during his sermons and would place his foot on their vaginas while they sat or lay down before him, or touch their breasts with his toes.

Despite the attitudes towards women endemic within the cult, children were discouraged, and many female followers were advised to take measures to prevent pregnancy, with some having abortions and others – men and women – even undergoing sterilization. One ex-member, Erin Roberts, recalled Rajneesh describing children as a distraction to the group's spiritual awakening and its members' relationship with him. Roberts herself was sterilized and recalled meetings she and other women attended, usually wearing very little clothing, in which Rajneesh would touch them inappropriately. Roberts also alleged that Rajneesh had sexually assaulted her.

Sannyasins were expected to complete months of therapy before they could apply for working positions in the ashram. None of the roles available were paid and overseers of the tasks were deliberately chosen for their harsh, aggressive personalities. The sannyasins were also made to believe that anyone outside the cult was ignorant, unworldly and unintelligent; in contrast, they were encouraged to see themselves as socially, culturally and, of course, spiritually superior.

As the years went on the ashram grew increasingly crowded, especially since some members remained there for years on end. Rajneesh asked his followers to locate a new property but clashes between the cult and Prime Minister

Morarji Desai prevented the granting of land-use approval and so the ashram was forced to remain where it was. The government increasingly attempted to curtail the influence and expansionism of Rajneesh's movement. It denied visas to foreign nationals planning to visit the facility and cancelled its tax-exempt status retrospectively, which resulted in a very high bill for Rajneesh. Controversy was beginning to mount. In May 1980, during one of his sermons, an assassination attempt was made on Rajneesh's life by a young Hindu fundamentalist.

In 1981, Rajneesh was hosting some 30,000 visitors a year, with the majority of audiences made up of Europeans and Americans. In April, Rajneesh, who was now known to his followers as Osho, decided to begin a three-year silent vow and his sermons were replaced with silent sessions spent listening to music and hearing readings given by other members of the cult. Osho also had a new secretary around this time, Ma Anand Sheela, who was previously known as Sheela Silverman. Osho claimed that when Sheela spoke, she was doing so on his behalf.

The tensions between Indian authorities and the cult were so fierce that Osho decided to set up elsewhere. The ashram was relocated in the same year to a ranch of 100 square miles in Wasco County, Oregon, and it was financed with £4.9 million of the cult's clearly sizeable coffers. It was here that Sheela was to prove so vital in the swift expansion of what she termed Rajneeshpuram, a whole new city dedicated to Osho and his teachings. Homeless people across the country were targeted in an effort to legitimize the new city and to provide more workers. Sheela was known to wield extraordinary power and could be harsh in doling out punishments to anyone who questioned or disobeyed her orders. She was deeply jealous, too, of anyone she regarded as too close to Osho.

In 1984, with county elections round the corner, a total of 751 people fell ill with food poisoning. Contaminated salad bars across ten restaurants in the city of The Dalles were found to be the cause and the perpetrators were members of the Rajneesh cult, who had hoped to incapacitate voters so their own candidates would win the elections. The attack represented the first and largest bioterrorist attack in United States history.

In the autumn of 1985, Sheela and several other followers fled the commune for Europe. Osho told press reporters that several crimes had been committed by his former secretary, but that he had not been aware of them. Scandals now erupted and all of them had Osho and Rajneeshpuram at their centre. There was immigration fraud, whereby sannyasins were accused of sham marriages in the United States in order to remain in the country, and the doctoring of elections by bringing in thousands of homeless "members" to help win county seats, who were then drugged with Haldol. In addition, there was the attempted murder of Osho's personal doctor.

Other alleged crimes included wiretapping and bugging within the commune and in Osho's own home. All of this, he claimed, was masterminded by Sheela, who was arrested in West Germany in October 1985. She was brought to the United States and pled guilty to first-degree assault and conspiracy to commit assault, arson and wiretapping. She was given three 20-year prison sentences, which were eventually reduced to four and a half years and to be served concurrently, and was fined almost half a million dollars.

Rajneesh himself was deported from the United States in 1985. More than 20 countries denied him entry and he eventually returned to Poona. In September of that same year, the Oregon community was destroyed by fire.

LUCK OF THE DRAW

Between 575 and 535 BCE, King Servius Tullius, the sixth king of Rome, came to believe his life was blessed. He was lucky, he felt. A popular king, he was one of the city's largest benefactors, enjoyed great success in battle against the Etruscans at the ancient city of Veii and during his reign expanded the city to include nearby hills. He enjoyed particular devotion from the lower classes of society, whose lives he was reputed to have improved. He is also credited with the creation of various festivals and possibly even the founding of Rome's first mint.

Finally, he ordered the construction of statues and of two major temples. One was dedicated to Diana, the goddess of the hunt, and the other to Fortuna, the goddess of luck and good fortune. It was the latter deity that the king believed responsible, almost entirely, for the success of his time as monarch. Sadly for Servius, this time was cut brutally short by his murder at the hands of his daughter, Tullia, an act that precipitated the fall of the Roman monarchy and the founding of the Roman Republic.

The once prosperous monarch is credited with an expansion of interest in and devotion to Fortuna. Her image and representation became more and more widespread across society and soon developed into a cult following that spanned the entire Roman Empire. In what became one of modern civilization's oldest belief systems, the Cult of Fortuna developed around the goddess. She personified chance and luck, and the growing believers in her ultimate power endured through to the Middle Ages and right up until the Renaissance.

Like other Roman gods and goddesses, Fortuna has a Greek equivalent: the goddess Tyche. Both were understood to be unpredictable, irregular and erratic; Fortuna is often portrayed wearing a blindfold, which represents her mysteriousness and connections to random chance. While we now understand the word "fortune" more positively, its older associations are more closely linked with both good and bad luck. Alongside the blindfold, Fortuna is also portrayed with a gubernaculum (or ship's rudder), a Rota Fortunae (or wheel of fortune) and a cornucopia (or horn of nourishment).

After Tullius' death, the cult was fairly diverse in its following, with lower-class citizens and royalty alike pledging their allegiance and worshipping the goddess. Over time though, the sect became increasingly associated with the aristocracy, particularly so for Emperor Augustus, who used his veneration of Fortuna to cement his position as the rightful leader from 27 BCE. Despite this shift, she remained a vital part of daily life for many ordinary citizens.

Not only did Fortuna command notions of luck and chance, but also those of fate. She was thought by many to have a direct impact on mortality, life and death, and in this guise she was known as Atrox Fortuna. In 23 BCE, Emperor Augustus was seriously ill: an issue made worse by the fact that he did not have a clear successor. He turned first to Marcus Agrippa and his nephew, Claudius Marcellus, and ultimately selected the more experienced Agrippa for the role. This may well have caused some political strife and tension, since Marcellus was the clear "blood" heir, but his death took him out of the race and Augustus chose Agrippa to be his daughter's husband. The pair had several children, including Gaius Caesar in 20 BCE, Julia in 19 BCE, Lucius in 17 BCE, Agrippina in 14 BCE and Agrippa in 12 BCE. To further consolidate his dynasty, Emperor Augustus adopted the two elder boys, Gaius and Lucius, as his own sons and heirs.

In 12 BCE, disaster struck when Agrippa, the emperor's right-hand man for 30 years, died. Panicked, the imperial administration now pinned its hopes on Gaius and Lucius, who were just eight and five years old respectively. Portraits, a well-practised method of propaganda at the time, displayed the boys as looking incredibly similar to their adoptive father, as ensuring the line of succession and cementing notions of ancestry were both vital.

Some years later, Augustus sent Gaius, who had by now completed his military training, to Armenia, where a revolt was taking place. Future rulers needed to cut their teeth early when it came to battles, wars and skirmishes, and so such an action was not especially unusual.

In 2 CE, Lucius was sent by Augustus to complete military training on the modern-day Iberian Peninsula; in mid-2 CE, he fell sick and died in Gaul. His death left all the emperor's hopes for succession pinned on the older boy. However, in 4 CE, Gaius also fell ill in Anatolia and died, leaving Augustus' lineage in tatters.

The exact causes of both deaths are unknown, though some contemporary historians believe the young men were murdered. Augustus was now heirless. In the aftermath, it was Atrox Fortuna, the fickle, changeable goddess, who was said to have claimed their lives. This theory gained far more traction than any notion of foul play and further served as a reminder of Fortuna's importance and the whimsy of her judgement.

In the years that followed, Fortuna's cult grew: devotees built temples and statues in her honour, notably in 293 BCE and 17 CE. People flocked from miles around to pay homage, much like contemporary religious shrines and the focal points of pilgrimages.

Followers also prayed to her for the safe return of Roman armies on military campaigns. Across society, she came to be associated with many different aspects of life: she was said to be related to the Matralia – goddesses of childbirth and fertility. Citizens of the lower classes developed a particular affinity with the image of a divine benefactress. She was a goddess, it seemed, for all. She could give or take away the gift of life, she could ensure a baby's delivery was smooth or complicated, and the strength of belief in her spanned classes and demographic groups. The Temple of Fortuna Virilis is found in the Forum Boarium at Rome, and is well preserved to this day.

Fortuna's longevity persisted despite the rise of Christianity in the second and third centuries. She continued to be depicted in artwork and through literature way beyond Imperial Rome. In fact, to this day the figure of Fortuna is common across Italian culture: the oft-used expression *la dea fortuna è cicea* translates as "luck is blind".

A TIMELY MESSAGE FROM HEAVEN

Visions of the Virgin Mary have been occurring around the world virtually since the beginning of Christianity itself, with the first instances taking place around 40 CE. The Roman Catholic Church has been investigating such accounts since 1531, when Juan Diego – who was of Aztec descent but had converted to Christianity – declared that the Virgin Mary had appeared to him and asked him to build a shrine at Tepeyac Hill, in what is now Mexico City. Since that time, many sightings and apparitions have been found, by the Church's standards and guidelines, to be legitimate.

It is no surprise that such visions play a huge role in the worship of saints and Christianity more generally. As the mother of Christ, Mary is regarded by some sectors of the Church as just as significant as, if not more so than, her Holy Son. Given that she herself was visited by an angel, the messenger Gabriel, she came to be associated with visitations, miracle-healing and divine announcements.

In 1989, sightings of the Mother of Christ became the focus of the Movement for the Restoration of the Ten Commandments of God, a cult that splintered from the Roman Catholic Church.

Based in Kanungu, south-western Uganda, it became notorious after 1,000 of its members were found dead in what was first believed to be the workings of a doomsday cult and was later revealed to be mass murder.

The years leading up to this religious sect's foundation had not been easy for Uganda. The brutal rule of Idi Amin had ended just ten years previously, and had been marked by civil unrest, persecution, war, nepotism and corruption, as well as numerous instances of human rights abuses.

Exact figures are hard to ascertain, but between 100,000 and 500,000 people are thought to have been killed under Amin. The period 1980–86 marked a conflict known as the Ugandan Bush War, a civil and resistance war fought between the government and the National Resistance Army among other rebel groups. In addition, rates of HIV in Uganda had been very high across the 1980s, as the AIDS epidemic took hold around the world.

As is so often the case, this environment led to a gradual disenfranchisement with the traditions of the established Roman Catholic Church, and several post-Catholic groups were formed around the same time as this next cult, the Movement for the Restoration of the Ten Commandments of God. Certain Catholic priests had been mired in scandal and for many ex-members of that Church it seemed as though the end of the world was nigh, complete with war, poverty and disease. Traditional religion, it seemed, was no longer the haven and sanctuary many had held it to be.

The founders of the new movement were Credonia Mwerinde and Joseph Kibweteere. Little is known about Mwerinde's past, but around the time of the cult's inception she largely earned her money through sex work, shopkeeping and brewing banana beer. Prior to the creation of her own church, she had been involved in a different religious group who worshipped the Virgin Mary, and it was here that she approached Joseph Kibweteere, wanting, she said, to repent of her sins.

Kibweteere had been born into a strong and fairly wealthy Catholic family; he had visited Rome in 1979 and built a church for his local community in the wake of the visit. He had also run for political office in 1980 and had donated some of his land to a Catholic school. He married a quiet, unassuming science teacher called Teresa, and the pair enjoyed a good and stable relationship. The couple started a family, and all seemed well.

Meanwhile, Mwerinde was likely travelling throughout Uganda in 1989, spreading the news of her visions in which she and her sister, Ursula, claimed to receive heavenly messages from the Virgin Mary. Followers clung on to Mwerinde's every word, with numbers growing by the month. It was because of the news of these visions that Kibweteere and Mwerinde first met, with the latter explaining how she could see the Virgin Mary within the stones of mountains nearby. Since Kibweteere had experienced similar visions, he welcomed her and it was at this stage that the new religion was founded. The bond between the pair was strengthened by their joint belief that they, and they alone, could help bring redemption to the mire of scandals and issues faced by the mother Church.

Over the next two years the group's numbers grew, likely through word of mouth among the deeply religious communities of Ugandan towns and villages. Several defrocked and excommunicated Catholic priests and nuns also joined the new sect, lending it enhanced credibility and legitimacy. If potential followers were unsure about joining, they needed only to look to the men they had for years considered their spiritual leaders. If they, too, seemed to agree that this was the correct path, it simply must be.

By 1991 it boasted 200 members and Kibweteere was named the ultimate leader, though it was suspected that Mwerinde held the most power and dictated much of her "wisdom" to Joseph to disseminate. She claimed to receive multiple messages from the Virgin Mary and sometimes spent whole days writing them down.

As the name of the group suggests, the key aims of the cult were to follow the Ten Commandments – the set of scriptures described in the Bible having been passed down from God to Moses on Mount Sinai. Some of the commandments, such as the prohibition on stealing or murder, were simple enough, while others were more challenging and open to interpretation.

The group's members were instructed not to talk, due to the Ninth Commandment's "Thou shalt not bear false witness against thy neighbour". Instead, they communicated in sign language. Unbeknown to the followers, this prohibition on speaking would have in turn prevented dissent or challenges to the pair's authority. It was a canny method of ensuring obedience.

Kibweteere's son Giles was extremely distressed by the change in his father, who he later told media: "loved us when we were children. But then he started to do whatever those women told him. He stopped loving us... They prepared nice food for higher ranks, but the rest could stay a day without eating. They would punish people. They would tell children not to go to school – including my brothers and sisters – and they would say the world was ending and that if we were sick we should pray instead of getting medicine."

Most importantly of all, though, Mwerinde and Kibweteere were convinced of the true reason behind the Virgin Mary's appearances to them both: to spread the word of the apocalypse, which was set to take place on 31 December 1999. For reasons that aren't clear, new members were even tasked with reading through the group's booklet, *A Timely Message from Heaven: The End of the Present Time*, not just once but six times.

Kibweteere is known to have sold some of his property, along with his car, in order to finance the resources required for the new recruits, which were growing steadily. In the meantime, tensions between him and his wife worsened, and reached a critical point when Ursula Mwerinde poured paraffin on a bag of Teresa Kibweteere's clothes and set it alight. She would go on to beat Teresa and Joseph did nothing to stop it.

Members lived alongside one another on banana and pineapple plantations and brought money raised by selling assets when they joined the cult. Primary schools and houses were built until 1992, when the Movement was ordered away from Rwashamaire, in south-western Uganda, and moved to Kanungu District, where Mwerinde's father gave the cult his own property for their new home. This was later renamed by the cult and became Ishayuriro rya Maria, or "the rescue place for the Virgin Mary".

Kanungu is a rural, isolated place. The nearest town is still 27 miles away, along a winding unpaved road. It has several thousand residents, but rates of sanitation are low and animals roam freely across the district. Sanitation has long been an issue for the region, and its inaccessible location makes improvements in this regard more complicated still. Much of the area is used for agricultural work, while the remainder comprises rainforest and bushland.

By 1997, there were some 5,000 members at the compound, despite reports of its involvement in the spread of disease caused by cleanliness, the kidnap of children and a use of child labour. One teenage member was quoted to have stated that the impending end of the world and the leadership's connection to God meant that believers in the group would be saved.

The dawning of the new millennium was, of course, the focal preoccupation of the group and its activities, especially as the time drew near. Members began to sell off their clothes and many who had left the cult in previous years were recruited once more.

Of course, the twenty-first century arrived without any sign of the apocalypse, which left its high priest and priestess with a crisis. The numbers of new members and donations plummeted. To combat the growing sense of unease and volatility among the members' ranks, Kibweteere and Mwerinde gave a new date for the end of the world – 17 March 2000. For many living in Uganda at this time, the apocalypse might have still seemed a likely scenario. The country had already suffered the brutality of Idi Amin, civil war and famine. In many ways, the doomsday they feared had already arrived.

As the new date approached, Mwerinde ordered all followers to burn what few possessions they had left. They were instructed to wash carefully in preparation for a party on the night in question.

At that party bulls were roasted and Coca-Cola was consumed. This may have seemed normal enough, but the festivities masked the true horror of what was to come. Unbeknown to the members, all the doors and windows of the building had been boarded up once they were inside.

Not all the cult's members were in attendance, however, with some still in separate headquarters in other small nearby towns. Around the same time as the terrible events unfolded at the party, other followers were poisoned, garrotted and stabbed. Their bodies were tipped into pits they had, it would later be established, dug themselves.

At the building Mwerinde called the "ark", the revellers remained unaware that there was some 1,036 litres of gasoline already stashed along with them all. Suddenly, the laughter and camaraderie at the party was cut short. A huge explosion engulfed the building and its attendees. Every single person was killed by the flames. Even those who might have survived the blast were unable to leave. In total, 530 people died. The group's two founders and other leaders were not accounted for and were thought to have escaped.

Police swooped on the grisly scene to find incendiary devices used to start the fire alongside the charred remains of the Movement's members. Over the following days they launched an investigation into its other properties, all spread across the south of the country. They discovered buried bodies at virtually all of them, including six in a latrine, 153 at a compound, 155 at a former Catholic priest's estate and a further 81 at one leader's farm. Some had been poisoned, others stabbed. The final death toll stood at 924.

To this day, there are international arrest warrants in place for both Credonia Mwerinde and Joseph Kibweteere. Mwerinde is believed to live in the Republic of the Congo. As for their motive, it became clear that the cult's leaders, sensing members' frustration and lack of faith after the failed doomsday prophecies, predicted an uprising and decided to use the new date of the "apocalypse" to wipe out the entire population of followers. A rebellion, they believed, would have been too risky and far too challenging to prevent.

A CAMPAIGN OF HATE

It was a regular morning for the parents, teachers and children at Sandy Hook Elementary School. In just a few short days the Christmas break would start, and the first graders were full of excitement as the morning began. Their 30-year-old teacher, Miss Lauren Rousseau, had worked across several different local schools before being offered a full-time post as a substitute at this elementary school. She had always wanted to teach; it had been her lifelong dream.

Just after 9.35 a.m., the previously peaceful morning was interrupted. Suddenly, the sounds of books being opened, pencils being sharpened and mental-arithmetic tests being puzzled over were replaced with gunshots, screams and bangs. Twenty-year-old Adam Lanza shot his way through the glass of the school's locked entrance door and quickly entered Room 8, Miss Rousseau's classroom. Armed with a semi-automatic rifle and ten magazines containing 30 bullets each, he began to fire. Rousseau, attempting to shield the children at the back of the classroom and then in a nearby bathroom, was shot and killed, as were 15 of her young charges. Just 5 minutes later, 27 people were lying dead – 20 of them children aged just six and seven – and Lanza turned the gun on himself.

In the aftermath of the horrific attacks, Sandy Hook Elementary School became the epicentre of renewed calls across the United States for tighter gun controls. President Barack Obama travelled to Newtown, Connecticut, to meet with the devastated families whose lives had been so utterly ripped apart in the space of just 5 minutes. And yet the following day the world was stunned to read, via social media, that a group was planning to picket the school and the vigil organized in the aftermath of the tragedy.

That group, who suggested God's judgement had been "executed" and planned to "sing praise" at the event, was the Westboro Baptist Church. Thankfully, swift public condemnations of the proposed picket kept Church members away. But the proposal itself was indicative of the group's response, and brought its reactions, tactics and belief system into harsh light.

The Westboro Baptist Church began as an arm of the Topeka-based East Side Baptist Church, formed in the early 1930s in Kansas. Twenty years later, a minister and street preacher called Fred Phelps was hired by the East Side Baptist Church as a pastor. On his promotion to a new East Side church called Westboro Baptist, Phelps removed himself and the congregation from the Baptist Church and established a small group of ardent followers.

For the next years there was little in the way of overt, publicized controversy when it came to the new sect, which described itself as "old school" and adhered to extremely rigorous readings of Calvinism. This branch of theological understanding saw all humankind as essentially sinful, with God as the universe's only benign and benevolent force. The majority of Fred Phelps' followers were family members, friends and close relatives, and in the entire history of the Church it has only ever had fewer than 100 members.

To this day, its headquarters are located in Topeka, in a fairly nondescript gabled house. The only giveaways of its activities are the tall black gates surrounding the compound and the signage on South West Cambridge Avenue: "godhatesamerica.com". Most members live in houses within the Church's compound, which includes a shared back garden.

For such a small group, the Westboro Baptist Church is nonetheless known and largely reviled worldwide. In the late 1980s it began to rail publicly against alleged homosexual meeting spots across the city of Topeka, and in June 1991 the first of its soon-notorious pickets was held in Gage Park, which Phelps claimed was a well-established gathering place for homosexuals. As the years went by, more and more such protests were held across Topeka and then even outside Kansas and the rest of the country.

It is significant to note that Phelps, born in 1929, would live through a century that experienced profound changes in attitude to sex, sexuality and gender. While he was cutting his teeth as a young pastor at the East Side Baptist Church, homosexuality was listed as a "sociopathic personality disturbance" by the American Psychiatric Association; in 1953, President Eisenhower's signed order banned gay people from working in government.

The start of the 1960s heralded a new change, as Illinois became the first state to decriminalize sexual activity between people of the same sex. Over the next decade, most eastern and western states would follow suit, but Kansas, Texas, Oklahoma, Alabama and Mississippi would not do the same until 2003.

During the early 1980s, Phelps could not have missed reports of the increasing numbers of men falling ill in what was one of the United States', and indeed the world's, largest healthcare crises of all time. As the AIDS epidemic spread, many strictly religious groups became further convinced of the legitimacy of their beliefs. To them, AIDS was a retributive act by a wrathful God, a means of enacting vengeance against the civil and LGBTQ+ rights movements being advanced across the less conservative American states.

The Westboro Baptist Church's first major public "outing" occurred in 1998, when it protested en masse at the funeral of a young gay man called Matthew Shepard. The 21-year-old student had been beaten, tortured and tied to a fence by two men in what was believed to have been a homophobic attack; he died from his injuries six days after the incident. Led by Phelps, the Church's members shouted abuse and held up signs on the day Matthew was laid to rest. Some of these read "Matt in Hell" and another – "God Hates Fags" – became emblematic of the hate speech set to define the group. So vitriolic was the tirade of abuse at the funeral that police were forced to create human shields between the Church and anti-picket groups attempting to protect the mourners.

Over the following years, Westboro's doctrines intensified in their opposition to all forms of homosexuality; any tolerance or inclusivity of non-heteronormative sexual activity was seen as an affront to God. As a result, the Westboro Baptist Church claimed that God had turned His back on America as a whole due to the increase in legalization of same-sex relationships and marriage.

A new campaign was initiated by Phelps in 1996. This suggested that certain attacks on Church members picketing were part of "Topeka's Baptist Holocaust", whereby members of the Jewish community and homosexuals had banded together to quash the group. Such anti-Semitic rhetoric brought the Church further condemnation but it continued to preach against Jewish communities, claiming they were responsible for increased legislation protecting those seeking abortion and those in favour of LGBTQ+ rights.

This hate speech soon extended to the funerals of soldiers who had lost their lives in Iraq and Afghanistan during the early part of the new millennium. The wars, Phelps claimed, were further evidence of God's wrath; the deaths of 4,500 servicemen and women were a punishment for the country's increased tolerance and perceived loss of morals. Despite their aggressive rhetoric and the distress caused to bereaved families, calls for the Westboro Baptist Church to be sanctioned or arrested for hate speech proved fruitless. The Church had even asserted that Barack Obama, two years into his term as president, was destined to go to hell and was in fact the Antichrist himself. However, since no immediate threats of violence or illegality were levelled at the president, the US Supreme Court stated in 2011 that citizens' right to free speech was paramount.

The majority of the group's funds appear to derive from lawsuit settlements. In 2006, for example, Albert Snyder, the father of a US marine killed in Iraq, sued the Church for defamation, invasion of privacy and emotional distress. Although Snyder was initially successful in his suit, the decision was later overturned and he was forced to pay the Church's legal fees.

Fred Phelps died of natural causes in 2014. Nine of his 13 children remain members of the Westboro Baptist Church, though some family members, such as his granddaughter

Megan Phelps-Roper, have since left and condemned its practices. Some have reported extreme methods of discipline used by Phelps, as well as beatings and a range of physical abuse. Countries such as the United Kingdom and Canada have subsequently banned members from entering.

It is unclear who, if anyone, holds the position of Church leader since Phelps' death but the group's activities – its messages of hate and homophobia, anti-Semitism, racism and conspiracy theories – appear to have been on the wane, and certainly less prominent, over the past decade.

POLITICAL, RACIST AND TERRORIST CULTS

For some cults, the sense of community and adherence to a strict set of social values and customs is enough to sustain the entire group, sometimes for decades at a time. They may share religious beliefs with other sects and branches, but recruitment of new members is not a priority and they might seem less concerned with challenging or changing perceived societal problems.

Political, racist and terrorist cults follow no such credence. In the main, they are focused on revolution, often by any means necessary. Theirs is a fight for perceived salvation, fuelled by notions of approaching catastrophe should their ideas be ignored. The battle, therefore, becomes all-consuming in the face of any legal or moral frameworks designed to prevent the actions they might plan for.

Many of the cults described in this chapter share the common themes of charismatic, charming leaders and a wholesale devotion to that individual's ideas. Where they differ from other types of cult is the lengths they are willing to go to: from paramilitary training to public denouncements, vandalism, weapons-hoarding, spying, terrorist threats and acts, and even murder. The nature of their motives is also, of course, a major distinguishing factor.

For cults of this nature, human beings become collateral damage in the war against the cult's established doctrines. There are many unwitting victims in the tales recounted in this chapter – people who were simply in the wrong place at the wrong time, or who, enticed by groupthink manipulation based on paranoia and fear, regarded their cult's reasoning as the only sensible option left.

In the aftermath of war in particular, these groups emerge as new legislation and reforms are passed to increase social cohesion. When the status quo is threatened – such as the dissolution of long-standing racial segregation or the assassination of a king or emperor and the installation of a republic – political, racist and terrorist cults proliferate, like ripples after a stone is dropped into water.

UNDERGROUND HELL

It was the morning of 20 March 1995 and the commuters of Tokyo piled on to the subway. It was a day like any other, bright and clear: the season was just turning and spring seemed ready to announce itself in earnest. Bankers jostled for space beside bricklayers, and schoolchildren fought one another over bags of technicolour sweets. Parents cast wary eyes on toddlers as the doors opened and closed, and the elderly sat waiting patiently for their stops, remembering the busy morning journeys they themselves had once made.

One young man started to rub his eyes: they were stinging. He must have caught a piece of dust on his way down on to the platform. The person next to him, a student by the looks of her, was doing the same thing. Funny, he thought. He wondered if the hay fever season was already upon them. And then he noticed others in the carriage doing the same thing.

One small boy was covering both his eyes with his tiny hands. The student released her grasp on the handrail and was violently sick, clutching her stomach as she heaved onto the floor. The young man scrambled to give her space while clasping his burning eyes; he heard a terrible sound, then a gasping, retching noise, and realized a mother with her two children in tow was turning a hideous shade of purple. She clutched at her throat, her eyes bulging.

Within moments, the ordinary morning had become a living nightmare. Up and down the carriage people began to shout and cry; the stench of vomit filled the air.

On that fateful day, 13 passengers died and almost 6,000 more were injured. Many went on to have debilitating health conditions as a result. But whatever had caused the devastation was invisible, hidden from view. It had crept on board along with them.

Authorities located five bags that were leaking by the time they were placed aboard three different train lines. Each was filled with the nerve agent sarin, which had been developed by the Nazis during World War Two. Sarin is both colourless and odourless, and lethal even at the lowest doses of exposure. Direct inhalation can lead to death as fast as a minute after the substance enters the lungs, and even in non-lethal doses permanent neurological damage is a strong possibility. This is a drug widely considered a weapon of mass destruction.

As police rushed to provide aid, the stricken passengers were slowly brought up to ground level and treated in makeshift shelters on the roadside by the underground stations. Newscasters rushed to the scene to capture images of the dead and injured – some were blinded, while others would never recover the use of their limbs and were paralysed.

The group responsible for the attack was a doomsday cult named Aum Shinrikyo. Its founder was Shoko Asahara, a man who claimed variously to be the first enlightened prophet since Buddha, and also Christ himself. Asahara was born Chizo Matsumoto in 1955, and grew up in an impoverished family in Kumamoto Prefecture. Having suffered with glaucoma since his birth, he was permanently blind in one eye and partially blind in the other. At his specialist school for partially sighted children he was remembered as a bully, often physically harming other children or taking their money.

Upon graduating high school, Asahara studied traditional Chinese medicine and acupuncture. The first years of his adult life were fairly unremarkable: he married and had six children, worked to support them and began to read widely on such subjects as Chinese astrology. In 1981, he was fined ¥200,000 (£1,100) for practising pharmacy without a licence, as well as selling unregulated drugs. His interest in religion and spiritual beliefs grew and he was involved in meditation and yoga, as well as esoteric Buddhism and Christianity.

Interestingly, this new fascination with religion was fairly atypical at the time among the general population of Japan, who still tend not to declare an affiliation to religious groups or belief systems, though a good portion of its society practises Shinto and Buddhism, often at the same time. By contrast, Asahara was searching for enlightenment through different ancient texts, exploring the path to this higher knowledge and understanding. For a time he was involved with Agonshu, a Buddhist group known for its belief in 1,000 days of offerings, in which participants agree to offer cash for the allotted time period – something Asahara himself completed. During this time, as he lived in a small flat in Tokyo with his wife and children, Asahara began to conduct free yoga sessions. As the weeks and months went on, he accumulated a small group of followers and started coaching them in the different schools of thought he had been learning from. It was a mix of Hindu and Buddhist beliefs, elements of Christianity, apocalyptic philosophies and occult practices, and word spread fast.

Followers believed that through Asahara they would be able to survive Armageddon, which would be brought about by an unspecified nuclear attack from the United States, an idea likely influenced by the 1945 atomic bombings of Hiroshima and Nagasaki. Asahara began to speak at universities, gathering further followers to his cause, and even wrote books. Aum Shinrikyo (Supreme Truth) had been born.

By 1989, Aum, as it was more popularly known, had been granted the status of an official religious organization and its following grew accordingly. It could now also boast a degree of independence from Japanese authorities, who were less likely to intervene in its activities after it attained its higher status. Students from some of Japan's most prestigious universities helped lend Aum further credence. Many had become disenfranchised by the notion that their academic careers would lead to profitable, secure jobs and here was a group that promised purpose, and a different, more intense salvation. The group now had 10,000 members domestically and 30,000 in Russia, perhaps as a result of the impending decline of the USSR and a resurgence in organized religion across that country.

Cult members who have since fled the group claimed that, despite calls to avoid materialistic pursuits, they were encouraged to pay for rituals during group ceremonies. These often involved Asahara's hair and even his bathwater. One follower paid £6,600 for an initiation that gave him a vial of the leader's blood to drink.

In 1989, 24 of the group's members attempted to run for political office in that year's elections, but none of them were successful. As a result, Aum began to develop sarin at its headquarters near Mount Fuji. The aim was to help members survive the nuclear attack that was to come: if they too had chemical weapons they might be able to launch their own attacks or prevent the apocalypse from happening altogether. As many of the group's members were educated scientists, their results were successful.

In April 1990, members collected soil from the Tokachi River basin in Hokkaidō and produced what they thought was *Clostridium botulinum*; they subsequently loaded three trucks with the substance and drove close to two US naval bases, Narita Airport, the Imperial Palace in Tokyo and the headquarters of another religious group, spraying the substance with a custom-built device wherever they went. While the hope was to cause mass incidences of often lethal botulism, they had not managed to isolate the toxin effectively and so the attack failed.

In March 1992, Asahara travelled to Zaire with around 40 of his followers. While the ostensible reason for the trip was to give assistance to Ebola patients, this was believed to be a front for the group's real intention of collecting samples of the deadly virus to disseminate it on Japanese soil. This was unsuccessful, most likely because the cult could not secure or transport the samples effectively.

The following summer, they made another attempt at spraying *Clostridium botulinum* at the wedding of Crown Prince Naruhito, and when this failed they attempted to spread the vaccine strain of *Bacillus anthracis* from their Tokyo headquarters. Once again, the attempt to cause mass civilian casualties – this time through anthrax – was unsuccessful, as they were unable to develop a usable strain of the toxin. It was clear, however, that the group wanted to further develop terrorist tactics.

Aum's first "successful" attack came in the summer of 1994, when perpetrators released sarin in Matsumoto using a heating pot and a fan to vaporize the nerve agent. There were seven fatalities and 144 people were seriously injured. The aim of the attack was to kill three judges who were in the process of bringing a fraud case against the cult, and it is believed the cost of developing, or attempting to develop, the chemical agents used in these attacks amounted to around £24.5 million.

From 1990 until the subway attacks in 1995, Aum was linked to 17 chemical weapons attacks. Four used sarin, four used VX, one involved the chemical phosgene, and the rest utilized hydrogen cyanide. In the meantime, the group is believed to have murdered 20 ex-members over the years of its key activity and carried out several kidnappings, mostly members of rival religious groups.

On the morning of the subway attack, the five members involved punctured the plastic bags inside their backpacks using the sharpened ends of umbrellas. They fled, and the chaos took hold. Some survivors reported a pervading smell of paint thinner before the dreadful symptoms of sarin poisoning commenced. "Liquid was spread on the floor in the middle of the carriage," one witness later told the press. "People were convulsing in their seats. One man was leaning against a pole, his shirt open, bodily fluids leaking out." When emergency services arrived, they had no idea what had caused the mass casualties and descended on to the underground platforms dressed in hazmat suits and face masks.

The attack represented a terrible shock to the Japanese people, as the country generally enjoys low crime rates and is seldom affected by acts of terrorism. Over the following years, the perpetrators and co-ordinators were arrested by police, questioned, and underwent trials. Two months after the atrocity, Asahara was found hiding in a crawl space at the cult's headquarters along with piles of money and a dirty sleeping bag.

Some members found to be involved were sentenced to life in prison, but Asahara himself was executed by hanging at a detention centre on 6 July 2018, along with 12 other key members of Aum Shinrikyo. The decision was supported by many victims and their relatives.

The subway attack also saw the creation of a new law prohibiting the creation of sarin and other agents, and increased power has been given to police with regards to religious groups and their activities.

After the mass attack in Tokyo, Aum was banned, fled its headquarters and went underground. In an attempt to distance itself from the subway attack, and since its leaders were largely in jail, the group changed its name to Aleph in 2000. It also agreed to pay a sum of money to the victims as compensation.

The group is thought to have around 1,600 members in Japan and under 500 in Russia and, according to some claims, the original teachings of Asahara are followed to this day, with members paying homage to his photograph and listening to recordings of his voice. The sarin attack in Japan's bustling capital remains the worst terror attack perpetrated in the country's history.

WHAT'S HAPPENED HERE?

As we have seen, times of strife are often a perfect fertile ground for radical thinking to emerge, and the 1930s in the United States are a good example. The nation had been economically ravaged by the Great Depression, prompted by the Wall Street Crash of 1929. Natural disasters abounded. In 1933, an earthquake ravaged California's Huntingdon Beach, killing 120 and causing huge damage. Forest fires devastated the mountainous regions of Oregon, while a dust storm whipped up the topsoil of South Dakota farmlands; by the following May, another storm had taken dust clouds 700 miles east to Chicago – a weight of 12 million pounds of dust was dumped by the wind. This was an era of crisis, in more ways than one.

To the average American, it must have seemed as though the world was coming to an end. A quarter of the nation's workforce were unemployed – almost 13 million people – and incomes had plummeted by half. It was into this bleak environment that Barbara Coe was born on a Sioux reservation in South Dakota, and it is very likely her family, on the Pine Ridge Indian Reservation, were impacted by the violent winds sweeping across the plains. It is unknown exactly when, but the family soon moved to Huntingdon Beach.

Astonishingly little is known of Coe's early life or teenage years, apart from the fact that as a young woman she was employed at the Anaheim Police Department, working as a crime analyst. Her story here begins in 1991, when she went to an office of the Orange County social services with a friend, and was astonished by what she saw. "I walked into this monstrous room full of people," she later stated. "Babies and little children all over the place, and I realized nobody was speaking English." This event appears to have launched her laser-like obsession with immigration across the United States: "I was overwhelmed with this feeling: 'Where am I? What's happened here?'"

In 1994, Coe was caught at work using a police camera to take pictures of striking Hispanic workers whom she suspected of being illegal immigrants. This appears to have been the turning point for Coe – she left or was sacked from her job and established the California Coalition for Immigration Reform (CCIR).

The unabashed aim of this political lobbying group was to deny access to public education and healthcare rights for any "undocumented" immigrants. This was in response to Proposition 187, otherwise known as Save Our State, which had gained traction among Californian voters in a referendum; several anti-immigration groups had supported the measure. During the Save Our State campaign, Coe had put up posters near polling booths bearing the slogan "Only citizens can vote". The FBI questioned her as a result, claiming she had attempted to intimidate arriving voters, but no charges were brought against her.

The autumn 1994 issue of *Rethinking Schools*, a quarterly publication focused on educational activism in the United

States, described how the then Governor of California, Pete Wilson, regarded the state's most pressing topic. "Wilson will tell you," read the article, "that California's problems have little to do with the recent recession, five years of drought, two major urban fires, riots, earthquakes, or the massive downsizing of the state's defense industry. No, these are minor when compared to the real villain: the illegal immigrant."

In 1995, Coe teamed up with Glenn Spencer, a hard-line anti-immigration activist known for lobbying for a "shadow Border Patrol" using civilians, surveillance equipment and even sensors to prevent migrants crossing the United States' border. The pair found themselves aligned ideologically and together they claimed to have foiled a plot brewing against the United States. The "Plan de Aztlan" was, they stated, a Mexican conspiracy aimed at achieving "*La Reconquista*", the supposed desire of Mexico to "reconquer" the country's seven south-western states. Spencer and Coe encouraged their growing numbers of adherents to organize rallies – usually on Independence Day – to draw attention to their demands.

At this time, members of the group aimed to reduce immigration and expand public awareness of the subject. While committed membership was small, with just 18 core members, the group's reach was wide. They managed to collect half a million signatures backing the ballot for Save Our State.

While the proposition initially passed, the bill was halted by California's new Democratic governor, Gray Davis, in 1998. Coe then used her own finances to erect a billboard at the California/Arizona border on Interstate 10, declaring the former to be "the Illegal Immigration State". Underneath this slogan ran the line: "Don't let this happen to your state." Coe denied that the billboard was racist but stated that any pushback against it was positive; she decried the "Hispanic pro-alien race activists". The board was only in place for a month before it was removed and Coe's money was refunded.

In 1998, Coe attended a rally hosted by the Council of Conservative Citizens, a white supremacist group founded 13 years prior that had created a set of core values, one of which "oppose[d] all efforts to mix the races of mankind". This represented another turning point in the cult leader's grim narrative, because before this point she had not worked openly with white supremacist groups. During the rally the Mexican flag was burned and speakers denied the Holocaust and made speeches against the country's Mexican and Asian communities.

Coe's rhetoric became ever more incendiary. She referred to all Mexicans as "savages" and "invaders" and claimed that George W. Bush was complicit in the country's attempt to use "illegal aliens" to conquer America. She also described Black people as "a retrograde species of humanity", and stated that "illegal alien children cause violence in our schools... they shoot, they beat, they stab and they spread drugs around".

As the years progressed the CCIR showed no signs of slowing down. In 2001, an "In Defence of America" rally at Anaheim's city hall turned violent – anti-immigration supporters clashed with Latino protestors in the streets. In 2006, some 14,000 Hispanic voters received mail sent on CCIR letterhead that advised that immigrants who were not yet citizens could not vote legally, and that should they attempt to do so they would be deported. The Department of Justice launched an investigation, noting that the attempt was clearly a manipulative tactic trying to dissuade Hispanic voters from involvement in the electoral system.

By 2008, clear evidence of societal change was cemented by the election of Barack Obama as the United States' 44th president, and the country's first African American to hold the office. Coe was vociferous in her criticism of the new leader, and in 2011 – after the killing of Osama bin Laden was announced – she claimed publicly that the president was lying and that he was, in fact, a Muslim himself. It is unclear why she believed the announcement to be a lie, or what significance Obama's faith might have had.

Her staunch belief in multiple conspiracy theories, coupled with the diatribes she became so well known for, appeared to have no limits. When one student, aged just 18, took his own life because he had not been able to secure legal, settled status in the United States, Coe described the situation as a "sicko yellow-belly coward illegal alien sob story".

Upon Coe's death from lung cancer in 2013, the group's influence was reduced. Coe's particular brand of cult leadership was deeply connected to her own image, personality and oratorical fervour, perhaps explaining why the group's activity tailed off so rapidly as she became older, suffered ill health and died.

Today, the group is known as the National Coalition for Immigration Reform. The Southern Poverty Law Centre, an organization dedicated to civil rights cases, maintains that the coalition still embraces its nativist legacy.

THROUGH THE MIND

In 1950, a former shipyard worker called Harvey Jackins agreed to help a friend. The man was known only as M, and he was desperate to avoid being committed to a mental health facility. Jackins had never worked in a therapeutic role – his previous jobs had mostly involved construction across his home town of Seattle, Washington – but he set about working with M, listening to his story, encouraging him to keep talking.

As the conversations progressed, Jackins noted that M would frequently shake, cry or laugh when he described some of his life's most painful episodes. And as time went by, Jackins was astonished to see the change in M: he regained some of his prior independence, seemed happier and calmer, and the looming prospect of treatment at a facility vanished.

Jankins decided to discuss the events of the past months with a group of friends and family. For the next two years, they met regularly to discuss formative experiences within their own lives and gradually developed a practice of encouraging one another to laugh and cry as they did so to fully express the thoughts and feelings that accompanied their stories. This became known as "emotional discharge". Believing he had developed a new therapeutic method, Jackins went to members of the psychiatry profession and attempted to persuade them to investigate the concepts he was developing. Unfortunately for Jackins, he was routinely dismissed.

For a time, Jackins was a close associate of the science-fiction author L. Ron Hubbard, who shared his belief in human growth and seeking one's full potential. Dianetics comes from the Greek word *dia* (through) and *nous* (mind). Hubbard created the concept and described it as the metaphysical relationship between mind and body, an idea since rejected by psychoanalysts as unscientific. When the pair began to disagree on certain elements of their ideology, they parted company and Hubbard went on to found the Church of Scientology.

Jackins then decided to resign from his job and set up a small office in Seattle. Personal Counselors Inc was born, a name that was soon changed to Co-Counseling – a switch born from the fact that two parties needed to be involved in the exchange of emotion and time spent listening to one another. The aim of his new venture was to "engage in, conduct and teach the art and science of Dianetics". The name was changed once more to Re-evaluation Counseling (RC) – it was believed that the process of talking and "discharging" in turn allowed followers to have new thoughts after the therapeutic session. It was seen as a two-way process that benefitted both parties.

The movement grew rapidly across the 1950s and 60s, and Jackins instigated a dissemination of his ideas and practices outside his native Seattle to the rest of the United States – specifically the East Coast – and abroad. Workshops were held every day, sometimes for hours at a time. The healing process was believed to involve many of the outward expressions Jackins had first witnessed with M, but now included "non-repetitive talking", "raging", sweating and yawning.

Children whose parents were active proponents of RC went on to describe upbringings where they, often as teenagers, counselled adults; people many years older were encouraged to divulge their most personal secrets, sexual encounters and memories. The disturbing nature of these revelations saw many experience post-traumatic stress disorder. Some recalled being held down by a group of adults and encouraged to scream.

All distress, Jackins believed, could be traced back to unresolved trauma, which could only be resolved with an egalitarian relationship between the counsellor and the client, who would switch roles and practise active listening to each other. The overriding belief system appears to have been a combination of Marxism, fighting social injustices and primal scream therapy.

In 1972, a leaders conference of RC's inner circle was held, and a set of guidelines were set forth by Jackins. This saw the implementation of "Regional Reference Persons", who would support leadership of the groups forming around the world. RC also developed its own method of certification for new teachers of Re-evaluation Counseling, and fees earned by such teachers were now taxed at 25 per cent to fund an outreach programme.

The group's materials were translated via audio and videotapes, and in 1976 the first World Conference was held. There were also elected representatives of marginalized groups such as gay members, Black citizens and women. Jackins himself wrote and published some 20 books across the course of his lifetime.

At first glance, the concept of Re-evaluation Counseling seems fairly benign. But the notion of psychotherapy as a key tenet of a group's core belief system is particularly interesting. When Jackins established his following, the United States and the Western world more generally were beginning to embrace the idea of open communication, self-expression and emotional intelligence. Previous decades dating back to the Victorian era had prized an avoidance of challenging emotional conversations. As time went on, the group was classified as a cult by many who saw its apparently omnipotent, charismatic leader as the embodiment of dangerous hero worship and centralized control.

Most followers of RC began with introductory classes lasting almost four months. Individuals were encouraged to find a partner to "co-counsel" alongside, and would then attend more workshops and support groups. Ostensibly the RC groups were keen to rid the world of oppression: Jackins oversaw the appointment of "International Liberation Reference Persons" for women, lesbians and gay men, the Jewish community, Black people and the elderly.

As time went on, RC-ers, as they were known, started to join and attempt to co-opt various civil rights organizations. Some members of Jackins' group infiltrated the Metropolitan Human Rights Center in Portland and encouraged pre-existing members to join their own therapeutic movement. Some were even elected to the highest positions of authority in LGBTQ+ advocacy groups, a fact made disturbing when Jackins' view seems to have been that homosexuality could not only be "cured", but should be.

In addition, members took positions at activist groups that campaigned for labour and social justice reforms, and were sometimes accused of trying to divert these groups' focus from the political agendas they had established to focus more thoroughly on personal growth. This saw a steady diversion of funds and time from organizations often run by volunteers, as members began to attend workshops focused on self-development and the discharge of painful emotions.

Jackins maintained throughout his life that the United States would always be fundamentally opposed to RC's "profoundly progressive nature and its effectiveness". Criticism has been levelled at the group for its mistrust of standard pharmaceutical treatments for mental illness. Despite RC's apparent focus on minority groups, it developed a "gay policy" that stated: "participation in sex with a human of your own gender is based on distress. It arises only out of distress experiences in the past." The group's doctrine on the matter claimed that "the distress out of which it arises" can be "completely discharged". Although Jackins retracted this original comment, it was reinstated in 1995 by the RC. Lesbians and gay men are still required to use pseudonyms when quoted in any RC publication.

A variety of claims were levelled at Jackins across the 1980s, when RC members accused him of several instances of sexual misconduct and rape, allegations that Jackins attributed to a slanderous dirty-tricks campaign by government agencies. Whatever the truth, little appears to have come of these accusations, and Jackins died in 1999. His son Tim was chosen at a conference of worldwide RC leaders to take the helm and remains an "International Reference Person" to this day. The RC's methods are used in 93 countries around the world, with some 1,500 teachers still practising.

SPLITTISH ACTIVITIES

Aravindan Balakrishnan was born in Kerala, on the southwestern tip of India. His mother had a curious instruction for him – warning him not to curse people, even when he was enraged. She informed him that he had supernatural powers, and she began to call him "Black Tongue".

At the age of eight, Balakrishnan moved to Singapore and met his father, who was working there as a soldier, for the first time. He was enrolled first at Raffles Institution and then at the National University of Singapore, where he was academically bright. It was here as a young man that he grew increasingly politicized. His growing support of communism was further developed through the state of crisis he witnessed, as rebels attempted to overthrow the long-held British colony of Malaya in the late 1940s.

Balakrishnan believed that Britain was a fascist state: he had witnessed the way in which native communities were treated in Singapore and, as such, his opinion of the country was low. He had observed cruelty, he later stated, including murder and torture. Nonetheless, in 1963 he was offered a British Council scholarship to study at the London School of Economics (LSE), and emigrated in the same year.

London was full of far-left fringe organizations at the time, many of which sought recruits from poor districts of the capital, which often had a higher proportion of immigrants. In that period, the arrival of Commonwealth migrants in particular had raised tensions among nationalist, far-right groups, and, just four years after Balakrishnan's enrolment at the LSE, the National Front was founded. While at university, Balakrishnan became heavily involved with student members of the Malaysian and Singaporean socialist and communist groups.

In 1967, Balakrishnan dropped out of university and joined the Communist Party of Great Britain. One former ally, Stephan Chang, recalled that over the following years his friend developed a "grand self-delusion that he was a great revolutionary leader, and he began to expose his extreme megalomanic, control freak and authoritarian characteristics".

As time went on, Balakrishnan's relationship with his student followers deteriorated as reports grew of his increasingly controlling personality. He was soon expelled from the Communist Party of Great Britain, accused of pursuing "conspiratorial and splittish activities" and "spreading social fascist slanders against the Party".

At this point, Balakrishnan created the Workers' Institute of Marxism–Leninism–Mao Zedong Thought. He gathered a select group of followers – one of whom, a Tanzanian classmate called Chanda Pattni, became his wife in 1971 – and persuaded them to take up his cause while beginning to publish the *South London Workers' Bulletin* from a squat house in the area. Balakrishnan's aim was to establish a "red base" in Brixton, an area of the city known for its ethnic diversity and large immigration population. He called on the Chinese People's Liberation Army, led by Chairman Mao, the communist leader and one of his political heroes, to "liberate" the district.

In 1976, Chairman Mao died and the group established a headquarters on Brixton's Acre Lane. Thirteen people – six of whom were asked to work and to hand over a portion of their wages to the group, another six of whom undertook full-time revolutionary pursuits, and Balakrishnan himself – lived at the converted bookshop, now named the Mao Zedong Memorial Centre. There was a huge portrait of Chairman Mao on permanent display, and his writings, along with those of Lenin and Marx, were all sold cheaply.

Balakrishnan started to call himself Comrade Bala and made frequent trips to the heart of London just two miles away, where he held public meetings attended by an increasing number of followers. One of the core tenets of his belief system was that China would soon conquer the world through a combination of technological spyware and satellite warfare. Flyers were distributed widely that featured a red-inked portrait of Chairman Mao in a worker's cap.

Members lived by a strict timetable of chores and were permitted to leave the residence in pairs only, as Bala, keen to instil a sense of fear in the group, stated that Brixton was notorious for violence. Once those in paid employment returned for the evening, they undertook shifts in the bookshop, listened to their leader's political rants, cooked and cleaned. By contrast, Bala spent days on end reading in his room. The women were often hit if they fell asleep.

The key members from this point onwards were Chanda, Josephine Herivel, a violinist from Ireland who had been educated at the Royal College of Music, Aisha Wahab, a Malaysian student and Sian Davies, a Welsh woman who gave the leader money to lease the shop. A former member recalled how joining Bala's cult was "like taking a nun's vows". Ironically, one of the seminars offered by Bala promised to teach attendees about "women's liberation as an integral part of the proletarian revolution". Bala encouraged the women to denounce one another to ensure that an atmosphere of fear and paranoia reigned supreme. One member was even encouraged to smash a bottle of her own perfume with a hammer to remove "bourgeois temptation".

The United Kingdom was on the precipice of great social change at the time. In May 1979, Margaret Thatcher was invited to form a government in Queen Elizabeth II's name, and her appointment caused a storm. She was the country's first female prime minister, and quickly instigated a series of reforms to privatize previously public industries, reduce the power of the trade unions, raise taxes and cut public spending. Interest rates stood at 30 per cent and unemployment soared. The perceived socialism of the post-war decades and the Labour government of the 1970s was over.

In the United States, the Republican administration of President Ronald Regan commenced, with a commitment to cutting income tax, the government's spending, and reducing regulation. This all stood in sharp contrast to Bala's Mao Zedong Memorial Centre, which was piled high with revolutionary literature and covered with Chinese flags. Bala's followers were encouraged to view the West with deep suspicion and fight back against the rise of the political right; they wore caps adorned with communist badges and held parties on Mao's birthday.

Bala had his Singaporean citizenship revoked in 1977 on account of the leadership of his new party; the Home

Office found he had participated in "activities prejudicial to the security" of Singapore. The group, undeterred by these findings, continued to reach out to London's working class and recruited new members to their cause.

When they outgrew their first premises, the group moved to a house in nearby Clapham. Bala and his followers claimed that the country was now moving in a "revolutionary direction" and aimed to combat the rise of fascism across the UK. As soon as 1980, their leader claimed, the People's Liberation Army would arrive from China to invade.

Bala gave frequent lectures and was often present at socialist protests, where he spoke to crowds directly. He claimed that he controlled the sun, the moon, the wind and fire, and that he alone would direct the subsequent overthrow of world governments, choosing who lived and who died. He told his followers about Jackie, an acronym for Jehovah, Allah, Christ, Krishna and Immortal Easwaran (an Indian-born teacher of spirituality), which was a sort of mind-control, thought-reading machine. He claimed that if any of the women even thought about leaving, the machine would wreak havoc on them and destroy them with lasers. He even attributed the failure of electric appliances in the house to Jackie's pernicious influence.

In March 1978, the group's headquarters were raided by police, who'd received a tip-off about drugs being taken at the house. Although none were found, nine members were arrested for assaulting the officers in attendance, with Bala among those detained. Since the members refused to accept the court's authority, they were all sent to prison briefly and the centre was closed down.

By 1980, the group had seven members, all of them women, and Bala took the group into hiding. Many former members with more liberal leanings had dispersed over time. For the following years they adopted an itinerant lifestyle, often moving around South London. Some of the cult's family members were described as "fascist agents", and the remaining followers were effectively exiled from communication with these supposed enemies. Bala often beat the women in his cult and four were sexually assaulted by him; they were forced to write detailed reports about their own sexual pasts, which he then read out publicly to the others in a "cleansing" exercise. The women also reported being forced to swallow his semen, which he termed "the elixir of life".

Astonishingly, the true extent of Bala's actions only came to light in 2013 when three of the women managed to escape the headquarters. It soon emerged that they'd lived as Bala's slaves for the past three decades and had endured unimaginable suffering in the process. Bala was arrested, charged and eventually found guilty, in a trial in 2015 lasting some three weeks, of rape, sexual assault, child cruelty, assault and false imprisonment. His crimes stretched all the way back to 1976. At some point during his fledgling career as a group leader, his political beliefs had morphed into a desperate need to control and subjugate anyone unfortunate enough to enter his orbit.

For years, Bala had managed to enact a campaign of manipulation and persuasion on the women living at his headquarters. He was known to shout, scream and beat them. He later "contextualized" his actions as a political necessity.

One of the escaped women was Katy Morgan-Davies, whose mother Sian had helped finance the bookshop in the 1970s. Bala had apparently claimed, without explanation, that her pregnancy was a result of electronic warfare. The girl was brought up to believe both her parents were dead and that

Bala was a deity. It is believed that the pregnancy came about in 1983.

After her daughter's birth, Sian Davies fell from a window in mysterious circumstances and was killed. In 2001, another member of the group, Oh Kareng, was said to have hit her head on a kitchen cabinet and subsequently died. One victim claimed that there was "no element of yourself that he [Bala] has left unexplored and that isn't open at all times to being humiliated and criticised." It was, she said, "like he takes a wire brush to your brain".

Bala was the only defence witness at his trial and claimed that when his leadership was challenged in the decades prior the result was the 1986 *Challenger* disaster, in which a space shuttle exploded early in its flight, killing all astronauts on board. He also claimed that Jackie had killed a former Malaysian prime minister and caused the election of Jeremy Corbyn as the Labour Party leader in 2015. Bala was sentenced to 23 years in prison. Just six years after the start of his term, he died there.

A CONFEDERATE OF HATE

On 9 April 1865, the Confederate Army of Northern Virginia surrendered to General Ulysses S. Grant at a small village courthouse. General Grant had led the Union Army of the north to victory over the pro-slavery Confederate states of the South, and would become the United States' 18th president in 1869. After four long years of battle and bloodshed, the American South was unrecognizable. Farms and factories had been destroyed in the fighting, roads were impassable and thousands of men had died.

In the city of Pulaski, Tennessee, a posse of six Confederate soldiers met in secret. The group they were about to christen would become one of the next century's most feared and reviled: the Ku Klux Klan. The name derived from the Greek *kyklos* (circle) and *clan* – a Scottish-Gaelic word that appears to have been written as "klan" for alliterative effect. Initially created as a social group of like-minded members, their movement would be a riposte to the recent surrender of their forces. Its intention was clear – the soldiers would gather others to their cause and enact a campaign of hate against Black communities.

After the Civil War, the system of reconstruction was introduced to rebuild and reform a society that had for years, in the south at least, relied on slave labour. To achieve this, a series of new freedoms and laws protected the recently freed slave population.

The Thirteenth Amendment to the Constitution was enacted, abolishing slavery and all forms of "involuntary servitude", except when a person was detained as a punishment for crime. It had been ratified as law by 27 of the United States' 36 members, at the time, and was the first of three major amendments to take place after 1865. Following the amendment, around 4 million slaves were freed from inhuman cruelty, persecution, forced labour, trafficking, rape and murder that dated back 100 years to the country's founding.

Over the next five years, two further amendments would serve to transform the social, political and economic landscape of the entire country. In 1868 African Americans were granted citizenship and in 1870 they were given licence to vote. This enfranchisement enraged certain sectors of the Deep South, where slavery had been the norm for so many years, and a large number of slave owners, ordinary civilians, farmers and businesspeople detested the new freedoms and liberties afforded to the Black population.

The Ku Klux Klan wasted no time electing a leader, and Nathan Bedford Forrest was declared its first "Grand Wizard". Forrest had served as a Confederate general during the war and was believed to have set in motion the grisly events leading to the Battle of Fort Pillow. This was fought on 12 April 1864, at western Tennessee's Mississippi River.

Forrest had commanded his men to massacre soldiers from the opposing side – many of whom were Black – despite the fact the latter had tried to surrender. The historian Richard Fuchs claimed that the battle represented "simply an orgy of death – for the vilest of reasons – racism and personal enmity". Although exact figures vary, it is thought that around 350 Black soldiers were murdered that day, 60 were wounded and 164 were captured.

Other prominent members of the new Ku Klux Klan were appointed as "Grand Dragon", "Grand Titan" or "Grand Cyclops". For many members, joining the cult gave them a sense of power and opportunity that, since their loss of the Civil War, had felt distinctly lacking. Within this new, special circle they found similar people and attained leadership roles.

From the beginning, the aim was to terrify. The Klan's members fashioned themselves cloaks and robes made from long swathes of material. This aided them further as they set out on their first night raids: with everyone dressed the same, identification of any one individual was close to impossible. Since much of the South was now occupied by federal soldiers, the group knew that evading capture was of the utmost importance. They set off into the night with the express aim of capturing and killing freed slaves, as well as any supporters who were giving them aid or who agreed with the amendment to the Constitution. The Klan referred to itself as an "invisible empire", which lent its members a sense of ill-conceived purpose and a patriotic hook on which to hang its hideous activities.

Over the course of just a few years, the group had grown markedly, moving from a small-scale fraternity establishing itself in secret to a terrorist organization determined to use any means necessary to stymie reconstruction. Myths and propaganda formed a large part of recruiting new members to the cause: members were told by the Klan's inner circle that their already shattered lives, following the Civil War, had been further ruined by the northern armies, Republicans and radicals. Their intent, they were told, was to completely overthrow the "legitimate" governments in place across southern states, and to elect "illiterate" Black councillors in their stead. As such, the KKK became a symbol of resistance, and was romanticized by many as the only hope the beleaguered southerners had to rebuild their lives.

Over the following years, the Klan would murder thousands across former Confederate states, indiscriminately slaughtering any Black southerner they came across and anyone thought to be an ally. In 1866, race riots erupted across Memphis and New Orleans, when white police attacked groups of Black civilians without any clear reason, and killed men, women and children alike with the support of supremacist mobs.

In 1868, the Klan published a set of "organizations and principles" stating its Christian values and its staunch patriotism. The questions asked of its members, however, placed it firmly within the category of white supremacy. The group asked its members for their views on Black political equality, the desirability of a white man's government, the emancipation of the white population of the South, the emancipation of southern white men, and the right for such citizens to protect themselves against unelected powers.

In that same year, elections were due to be held. The state of Louisiana had published its new constitution, which included voting rights for black men: in order to be readmitted into the Union, it had been required to enact this right to suffrage based on the 1867 Reconstruction Acts. Black voters had elected Oscar Dunn, a Black Republican, as lieutenant governor, and the Klan ramped up its deadly activities to intimidate Black voters.

POLITICAL, RACIST AND TERRORIST CULTS

The Klan was not the only white supremacist cult spreading its message of hate during this time. The Knights of the White Camellia (1867) was another secret group, as, later, were the White League (1874) and the Red Shirts (1875). However, the Klan emerged as the primary instigator of terrorism based on its opposition towards equality. They now wore hoods, again to conceal their identities and provoke fear, and rode through the southern states beating and killing would-be voters. Kansas saw 2,000 politically motivated murders and Louisiana around 1,000, with Georgia also a frequent target of the Klan. Many of these so-called "campaigns" saw Black people tarred and feathered, raped and even lynched. With their burning torches held aloft and their white sheets billowing out behind them, the Klan were soon an object of fear and horror to many southerners, Black and white.

The violence was both so immediate and so widespread that, in 1869, its first leader, Forrest, ordered the KKK to disband. This call was accepted by some factions and local branches, but ignored by others, and in 1871 the US Congress passed the Ku Klux Klan Act, which allowed the government to try to prevent the cult's attacks and arrest its members. This resulted in nine counties in South Carolina being placed under martial law and many members of the group being arrested.

This was regarded as the Klan's "first era". The Compromise of 1877 was a political deal intended to garner support from the South in presidential elections, and it involved the US government withdrawing troops from the southern states. As a result, these state governments enacted "Jim Crow" laws – named after a blackface character in popular "minstrel" theatrical shows of the nineteenth century – which enforced community segregation. All public services were now separated between Black and white civilians, from schools to public transport and even water fountains. In 1896, the Supreme Court set forth a doctrine of "separate but equal" when it came to the rights of African Americans. As a result, the Klan saw itself as being both sanctioned and legitimized in law.

By 1915, the Klan had expanded the focus of its hate and, in one infamous case, murdered a Jewish factory superintendent called Leo Frank. It now called itself the Knights of the Ku Klux Klan and was vehemently anti-Semitic, anti-Catholic, anti-communist, anti-immigration and xenophobic. The Klan's second phase had begun, and branches spread from the South into the Midwest. In 1925, it is estimated that the group had some 4 million members; they staged a march in Washington, DC – a far cry from the secretive underground organization of the 1860s.

The Klan expanded its remit to include strict methods of "social vigilance" during the 1920s, targeting Protestants, "immoral" civilians of any race, "traitors", girls caught riding in cars with men, and divorcees. In Georgia, a woman was subjected to 60 lashes for the charge of "immorality and failure to go to church". When her 15-year-old son attempted to help her, he too was lashed. This fresh focus on upholding conservative nuclear-family values and traditionalism proved ragingly popular. It charged a joining fee of $10, which was tax-free as – ironically – the KKK was regarded as a charity or "benevolent" society.

During the civil rights movement of the 1960s, the Klan became a prominent force of opposition once more. For the prior 40 years its presence had not been as visible, largely because it had considered its work complete. Now, however, it escalated once more and began a fresh campaign of murder and bomb attacks.

POLITICAL, RACIST AND TERRORIST CULTS

On 15 September 1963, four members of the United Klans of America, another offshoot cult, planted sticks of dynamite under the steps of a Baptist church in Alabama. When the dynamite exploded, five children were busy changing into their choir robes in the church's basement: four of them were killed by the blast, with one being decapitated. Addie Mae Collins, Carole Rosamond Robertson and Cynthia Dionne Wesley, all 14, were killed alongside 11-year-old Carol Denise McNair. Around 25 others were seriously hurt in the explosion; Collins' sister had 21 pieces of glass embedded in her face and was left blind in one eye. Martin Luther King Jr would describe the event as "one of the most vicious and tragic crimes ever perpetrated against humanity".

As a result of these increasing acts of terrorism, many Black Americans fled the southern states. The Great Migration, as it was known, involved the movement of over 6 million Black Americans over a six-decade span, and by 1970 just under a fifth of the entire population in the South was Black. The following decades saw a merger of neo-Nazi hate groups and pre-existing Klan branches into a larger and more dangerous white-power movement.

The Klan also targeted Hispanic communities, Asian and Native Americans, Muslims, Catholics, drug dealers, nightclub owners, members of the LGBTQ+ communities and providers of abortions. Klan membership stood at around 10,000 by the end of the 1970s, but the number of people who sympathized with the cult's cause yet weren't members themselves stood at a staggering 75,000.

By the 1980s, the KKK was in decline and the US government attempted to curb the now 120-year-old cult by prosecuting its different factions. This led to a reduction in members, and the violence witnessed particularly in the latter part of the nineteenth century decreased markedly. However, the group vocally criticized employment policies and welfare programmes brought in by the government and declared there were multiple plots being constructed by Jewish communities to "mongrelize the white race".

Specific figures of current membership are not, due to the very nature of the KKK's secretive operations, an exact science, but there are believed to be around 40 Klan groups active across 22 states to this day. This number increased in 2017, a year after the Republican Donald Trump took office. It wasn't until 2020 – in the wake of widespread, multinational calls for a re-evaluation of past figures and their celebration – that a bust of Nathan Bedford Forrest, the first KKK leader, was removed from Tennessee's state capitol building after a commission voted on the matter.

THE FASCIST AGENDA

While many cult leaders develop a fixed, immutable ideology and deviate little from it during the course of their "reigns", there are some whose belief systems change like the wind. In 2019, political cult leader Lyndon LaRouche died in prison at the age of 96. Across the course of his life, he would move from the far left all the way to the far right, and his followers – LaRouchies – became mainstays of reactionary, conspiratorial political movements across the 1970s and 1980s.

LaRouche was born in 1922 in Rochester, New Hampshire, to orthodox Quaker parents who had converted from Catholicism; the family later moved to Lynn in Massachusetts. As a child, LaRouche was badly bullied and identified as a loner, isolated from his peers and reading widely, particularly philosophical texts. The family experienced an upheaval in 1940 when Lyndon's father was expelled from the Quakers for accusing other members of misappropriating funds; both Lyndon and his mother resigned in solidarity.

From 1948 until 1963, LaRouche was a member of the Socialist Workers Party. During this time he graduated from Northeastern University in Boston; as World War Two erupted around him he joined a Civilian Public Service camp, which provided conscientious objectors like LaRouche with an alternative to military service. He then joined the army as a non-combatant member and travelled to India and Burma with the military's medical teams. After the war ended, he worked as a management consultant in New York, married a psychiatrist called Janice Neuberger and had a son in 1956.

His early years were characterized by a staunch belief in Trotskyism, which advocated for the emancipation of the proletariat over the bourgeoisie, mass democracy and the notion of "permanent revolution". It also condemned the regime of Joseph Stalin in the Soviet Union.

As the 1960s came into full swing and progressive ideals flourished, LaRouche began to associate with radical student groups at Columbia University and found particular favour with the Progressive Labor Party, described by some commentators as Maoist. He established the National Caucus of Labor Committees (NCLC) and by 1973 the group had 600 members. Part of his initial campaign was to encourage his supporters to attack other left-wing organizations and Communist Party members to emerge as the clear front runner in the fight against capitalism. It was known to promote a "socialist re-industrialization" of the US economy and proposed confiscatory taxes on investments perceived as wasteful.

At the same time, LaRouche began a series of meetings among members that were designed to denigrate and humiliate them, much like the public shaming and denouncements seen at the height of Chairman Mao's rule during the Cultural Revolution in China. This focus on terrorizing his subjects psychologically was key to ensuring their co-operation; LaRouche convinced many followers that he was being closely monitored by the CIA and that it was likely a close supporter had been "brainwashed" into planning his murder.

During this time the NCLC was known to have associated with the Ku Klux Klan, and it accused the Communist Party in the USA of plotting to attack it. In 1974, an "officers training camp" was opened in Argyle, New York, and followers were trained to use nunchakus, a Japanese weapon.

It is challenging to define exactly what the NCLC was fighting against at this stage: it had moved its position so fundamentally and in such a contrasting way that specific doctrines were contradictory or wildly outlandish. In essence, LaRouche's fundamental belief was that all of civilization could be described as a war between Platonists (followers of the philosopher Plato, who believe in an "absolute truth") and Aristotelians, who believe in relativity.

Scholars have since defined LaRouche as adhering to the philosophical idea that all human endeavour ought to bring positive benefits to the world. To LaRouche, the Aristotelians were delinquents bent on the world's destruction through permissive social, sexual and cultural movements, which would in turn see power handed over to the very richest, leading all nations into a new Dark Age. LaRouche soon became known for developing increasingly bizarre conspiracy theories – a key tenet in defining cult status of a group – and, more disturbingly, convincing his followers of their veracity. Some of his wildest claims involved Queen Elizabeth II, whom LaRouche decried as a global drug trafficker, the Bush family – who had collaborated with the Nazis between 1939 and 1945, according to LaRouche – and the Holocaust, which he denied had ever occurred.

In 1976, LaRouche ran for presidential office as the candidate of the United States Labor Party; over the course of his life, he repeated the process seven times. His campaigns, though unsuccessful, were publicly funded through federal matching schemes that brought him just under $500,000. His followers' donation sums were large, but LaRouche had also founded three separate companies, which brought in some $5 million per year. Sales of the group's magazines and literature also raised money.

The organization now had around 1,000 members, 37 offices across the country and 26 more in Europe and Latin America. In 1986, two of his followers won the Democratic nomination for lieutenant governor and secretary of state in Illinois. At the same time, LaRouche set up a network gathering private intelligence, where supposedly sensitive information was passed between different agencies and rival groups.

As the 1970s wore on – and despite professing to despise Adolf Hitler, the famously anti-Semitic composer Richard Wagner and other high-profile anti-Semites – LaRouche pulled back from Marxism and began to fraternize with neo-fascist, far-right groups. He frequently travelled to what was then West Germany, began to declare that the enemy of all mankind was the Rockefeller family and set up meetings with anti-Semitic groups such as Liberty Lobby.

The latter was a think tank founded in 1957 that touted several anti-Semitic conspiracy theories, denied the Holocaust and broadcast their views on a radio show that was aired every day. LaRouche also publicly defended the Nazis, claimed that Jewish people were "intellectual pus", and put forth the idea that Israel's actions on the world's stage were "a hundred times worse than Hitler". This was particularly problematic for his members, not least because 25 per cent of them were Jewish.

Many of the LaRouchies were highly educated academics, some with multiple degrees from excellent universities. As such, LaRouche was able to access politicians, journalists and public figures by utilizing an expanding contacts book. Bobby Inman, a former admiral in the navy and a deputy director of the CIA, had been in touch with LaRouche and had been offered information about political parties abroad from LaRouche's travels.

As LaRouche's popularity grew, so too did his public image. Despite his increasingly strange theories and ideas, the media appears to have presented him as a harmless eccentric rather than the more dangerous cult leader he had actually become. When new members joined his posse, they were encouraged to beg, borrow or steal money from their families before isolating themselves, to borrow to the maximum on credit cards and take out bank loans. All of this was then funnelled back into the NCLC. Since LaRouche had developed a reputation for being litigious, however, there were comparatively few exposé pieces or scoops about him or his followers when compared with other cults of this nature.

He developed ties with many seemingly disparate organizations, from farmers and abortion opponents to Klan members and the Black nationalist group Nation of Islam. Sympathizers handed out his writings in airports and richer members of society from different walks of life donated handsome sums to the cause. Many bought into LaRouche's credo that he alone could prepare the world for nuclear war and mass starvation, and prevent the apocalypse that was coming, perhaps as a result of the rise of Aristotelian values and politics.

In the mid-1980s, LaRouche and his followers moved to what he called Ibykus, an estate in the sleepy rural countryside of North Virginia. Their leader was convinced by this point of his impending assassination by Libyan hitmen, Soviet spies or drug dealers. The compound was heavily rigged with security measures and his followers walked the perimeter with semi-automatic rifles. "We feel if we rock the boat, they could get nasty with us," one local reported to the *Washington Post*. "We have to coexist with them, but we don't agree with their political beliefs." Residents were both perplexed and alarmed by the arrival of the cult, with no idea as to what LaRouche was trying to do, or why.

In 1987, LaRouche was investigated by the FBI and charged with fraud, against both the Internal Revenue System (IRS) and supporters who had loaned him a combined total of over $30 million. For this fraudulent fundraising he was sentenced to 15 years in jail but was released in 1994 after serving just a third of the sentence; two years later, he ran for president again. When Barack Obama took the White House in 2008, LaRouche made several claims about the president's likely assassination by undisclosed members of the "British Empire".

To this day, we can see elements of LaRouchian philosophy in the proliferation of fake news and misinformation, and the legacy of LaRouche has given rise to other politically minded conspiracists. While the cult has certainly seen its members diminish in the years since LaRouche's death, it was involved in racist rallies following President Obama's inauguration.

The question of how individuals like LaRouche gain so much traction may seem baffling, but cult expert Catherine Picard says the answer is simple: it's how a group presents itself. "This movement bases all its arguments in politics," Picard says. "It is not a political movement, it is a cult movement."

THE HOLY GRAIL

The Grail Movement came into being in late-1940s Germany, in the aftermath of World War Two and the devastation it caused around the world. This spiritual organization stands out because it was established not by one "omnipotent" or charismatic leader, but by its members themselves. The group's key mission was to spread *In the Light of Truth: The Grail Message*, a series of lectures concerned with the nature of human existence, the purpose of life and how to achieve spiritual harmony.

"I wish to fill the gaps which so far have remained unanswered in the souls of men as burning questions, and which never leave any serious thinker in peace," wrote its author, Oskar Ernst Bernhardt.

Bernhardt was born in the town of Bischofswerda, in what was then the German Empire, in April 1875. He began to write from a young age while living and training to become a businessman in Dresden and had already published several books by the time he came to *The Light of Truth*; these included *The Bracelet*, *Annita*, *The Adventurer* and *Diamonds*.

Many of his works were travel stories or plays, and some contained thinly veiled political comments or reflections on modern life and the hypocrisy Bernhardt witnessed therein.

He travelled widely in his youth, and voyaged to New York in the early stages of World War One; records reveal that he was arrested in the city – for what exactly is unknown – and he was interned on the Isle of Man in 1915. During his four-year imprisonment he wrote further and claimed that he experienced visions of his past life as Moses. On his release in 1919, he returned to his home country.

In 1928, he was residing in the mountainous region of Vomperberg, western Austria, and it was here he is believed to have taken the thoughts and ideas percolating during his imprisonment and turned them into *Im Lichte der Wahrhei (In the Light of Truth)*. He published the work under a pen name – Abd-ru-shin (Servant of the Light). It was an instant success upon publication and readers flocked to Vomperberg to take up residence near its author. Newspapers described how Bernhardt now called himself the Messiah of the Tyrol, and the Prophet of Vomperberg.

The new arrivals soon set themselves up with new homes along with a town hall and work sheds, temples and festival arenas. More followers of the Grail Message appeared throughout the latter part of the 1920s and well into the 1930s. Their tract of land was thought to be the location of Abraham's biblical vision of the mountain of salvation. Religious services were accompanied by classical music and lectures given by Bernhardt, who appears to have lived among his followers without incident during this time and who led the Sunday services at the group's own hall.

The Grail's followers worshipped the God of Christianity as "eternal light" and believed that all humanity could be categorized as "spirit germs", as everyone possessed the potential for reincarnation. Followers also believed in gnomes, elves and sprites, the latter being supernatural creatures similar to fairies. Once a new member underwent the initiation, a "sealing" ritual that bound them to God, they became "Crossbearers". There was no physical grail as such, but followers saw it as representative of a power transfer between humans that could only be retrieved by divine prophets like Bernhardt.

The book's foreword set out his vision, criticizing religious fanatics and the prejudiced, and arguing that a divine message would lead all truth seekers from the confusion of the modern world. Bernhardt emphasized the power of such truth to enable followers to find the right path.

By the mid-1930s, however, the political atmosphere was intensifying. In 1938 the Nazi Party annexed Austria and seized control of the cult's compound; all residents were expelled and the German soldiers took the area of land for a training camp. Residents had been planning for the construction of a marble temple called the Grail Castle, intended to hold 22,000 followers of the new religion. Instead, Bernhardt was arrested on charges of "infracting currency laws" and sent to prison in Innsbruck; he was released but subsequently re-arrested by the Nazis for illegally exchanging German to Austrian currency.

Two years later the country was occupied formally by the German army and Bernhardt was arrested once more. Hitler outlawed the cult and banned its literature. This time Bernhardt was exiled, to Kipsdorf in the Ore Mountains of Saxony, and was forbidden by the Gestapo from talking about the Grail or engaging in any sort of writing. When he was finally released in 1941, he was placed under house arrest in Kipsdorf. It is unclear how, but he died while under surveillance in the same year.

It wasn't until the end of the war that the Grail Movement was reborn. The Allies gave the compound back to Bernhardt's wife, Maria, and news of Abd-ru-shin's book and its teachings spread quickly once more. Some followers believed that Maria and her daughter, Irmingard, were the divinely chosen natural successors as the group's leaders.

Here, in the writings of the late author, devotees found answers to the terrible questions raised during the six years of World War Two. Here was everything from divine justice to free will, life after death, fate, karma and teachings about Jesus' mission on Earth, plus reflections on ancient myths, legends and modern art. The work also contained information about the Holy Grail and described it as the connection between God and His creation.

Over the following years, a large and devoted group of followers amassed across Europe. In the wake of the war, there was perhaps a greater appetite for the notion of spiritual growth and achieving a higher plane of consciousness: Abd-ru-shin claimed that if they committed to it, humans could create an earthly utopia by adopting his own lifestyle and appreciating nature for the wonder it was.

The membership spanned 16 countries in Europe but it was especially active in Germany and France. There were hundreds of followers in both the UK and the USA, as well as Canada, Brazil, Ecuador, 22 countries in Africa, Australia and New Zealand. In 1990, the Grail Movement split into two groups; Bernhardt's daughter had stated in her will that her father's books and lectures were to be left to the International Grail Movement. This decision angered other members of the family and led to the creation of independent branches of the Crossbearers, which appear to have functioned without incident for many years.

That was until 2008, when a new father decided to put in a baby monitor at his home in Brno in the Czech Republic. On plugging the device in, he was horrified when the signal picked up footage from his neighbour's monitor. The image showed a naked boy chained up in the cellar. Police descended on the home of Klara Mauerova, who was found to have kept her two sons Jakub, ten, and Ondrej, eight, locked in the cellar. She described how she and two friends had joined the Grail Movement; one of her friends' fathers was a "doctor" in the cult, and had instructed her to keep the boys in cages, whip and beat them, sexually abuse them and, most horrifyingly of all, partially skin them.

It emerged that the three women had committed cannibalism by eating some of the boys' raw flesh and even forcing the children to do the same. The women fled but were eventually captured and tried, while the boys were – thankfully – placed into care. The adults claimed during trial to have enslaved the children to "break" them and ensure their loyalty to the cult forever.

In the same year, the leader of the Brno Grail Movement was arrested after it emerged he had enslaved a group of women at his property. They had all been forced into manual labour and were denied all but the merest portions of food; one woman had died and was buried on the compound. The Grail Movement denied associations with either of these scandalous crimes and claimed they were the work of unrelated sects that had branched off from the original movement in the 1990s. It is believed that 10,000 members of the Grail Movement still exist across nations in Europe and Africa.

THE GREEN REVOLUTION

In 1973, a Canadian man called Pierre Maltais founded La Tribu (The Tribe). Maltais was, he claimed, of Mi'kmaq descent and could trace his ancestry back to Canada's Indigenous native peoples.

La Tribu was an ecological group dedicated to preventing climate change, the destruction of woodland and rainforest, and the advocacy of using natural products. They were opposed to the ultra-processed, mass-produced foodstuffs they observed had become the norm for most Westerners and rejected modern medicine. They were based in Paris from 1978, where they sold hand-crafted artisan items using only natural ingredients – six years later, they set off on a world tour to spread their message, plant trees and recruit new members. They eventually settled in Sweden, with Maltais serving as a shaman figure for the 30 men, women and children who followed him around the globe.

The group's original followers were mostly French, Belgian and French Canadian. They soon gathered interest as they dressed in traditional tribal costumes and took new names inspired by Indigenous tribes. La Tribu's own name was soon changed to Ecoovie (roughly translated as "ecological life"), and then again to Iriadamant (translated as "lifestyle painters").

In the autumn of 1991, the group arrived in Finland having walked all the way from Italy. Erkki Pulliainen, an architect and a professor of zoology at the University of Oulu, praised the group's work. The professor was a member of Finland's Green League and lent the group his financial backing to "study living in nature". This experiment was called the "Ecological Sylvilisation and Survival with the Aid of Original Cultures" or ESSOC project, and the Iriadamant were granted a one-year residence permit to study how humans adapted to living as native civilizations had once lived, and to observe the natural Arctic landscape. The group had been in contact with several municipalities in Finland to ascertain their suitability.

It was initially decided that the Iriadamant would conduct these experiments for seven years, after which point, Maltais hoped, they would live sustainable lives without the aid or interference of modern civilization. The initial press release describing the project's aims stated that it was "purely scientific" and focused on survival in Finnish conditions with the plants that nature provides throughout the year and the effects of Indigenous methods for tending the soil on the forest's rotation cycle. Members would also draw up a roster of survival techniques for the future, testing subsistence farming and construction in preparation for an ecological disaster.

It was hoped that the research gathered by the Iriadamant could be collated on to cards and subsequently published more widely – the Finnish National Agency for Education was a collaborator on the proposed research. It was even planned that schoolchildren would be taught some of the group's learnings within the national curriculum for the year 1994–5.

The Iriadamant established a camp near Kittilä, in the north of the country. Their plan was to later relocate to the south, but the first location was chosen because the group agreed to visits from tourists. Located within the Lapland area, Kittilä has a population of just 6,500 and is the coldest area in Finland: it reached −51.5°C just eight years after the group's arrival. It is a strange, other-worldly place, full of polar bears, caribous, wolves, whales and ptarmigans. From the end of May until mid-July the midnight sun hangs above the horizon and then, for two weeks in December, the polar night descends, when nights last for more than 24 hours at a time.

Despite the fact that the group's members were European, they were known as *Kittilän intiaanej* (Kittilän Indians). Unlike the new arrivals of other cults, the clan were originally welcomed and their mission was regarded positively both by residents and – when the phenomenon was reported – the wider country. The group constructed a marketplace and houses called *gwans*, which they covered with turf; men, women and children were all housed separately. They would, it was promised, gather their own food and live on a vegan diet of plants, seeds, pulses and fruit.

One of the Iriadamants' core beliefs was the concept of animism: the idea that animals, nature, weather, objects and places have a spiritual heart. The group engaged in daily rituals and routines that followed the rhythmic cycles of the seasons and planets. It established "guardians of the elements" through elections; their responsibility was to plan and structure the day's tasks for other members. Certain members also left the compound occasionally to give lectures on sustainability and primitive living in towns and cities around Finland.

Each day, members of the cult performed a sun salutation and welcomed the new day before starting on their chores. In the afternoon, drums would gather the community together to present the food each follower had found in a ceremonial fashion. Followers were encouraged at these occasions to craft gifts for one another made from the natural resources they came across in the wilderness. The remainder of the day involved preparing the commune's one meal, eaten at 6 p.m. in a circle. After the dinner, the Iriadamants would sing and play music round the campfire and socialize together.

For the first year of the experiment, some 100 followers gathered beyond the Arctic Circle, determined to live primitive lives and develop their own language, culture, music and festivals. Those who had not joined the research project in this harsh, desolate environment were nonetheless ardent supporters of the cause and there were some 500 members spread across Europe in the first years of the 1990s. A similar camp was even established in Italy.

Within a year of their arrival, though, the Iriadamant closed its doors to outside observation and the tourist board, with whom it had agreed to co-operate. Newspaper reports began to emerge about the issues residents were experiencing with the group, and with police. It appeared that the idealized state of self-sufficiency had not been attained and farmers were donating food to starving cult members. Potatoes were also smuggled into the camp illegally when it transpired their own crops had failed. Every day, four trucks took firewood into the compound.

Although modern tools were banned, it emerged that contemporary kitchen items were being disguised to look like they were made of wood and modern saws were used to cut down trees. Years later, when the camp was examined thoroughly, a great deal of plastic waste was discovered.

In August 1992, it was reported that a child of three had died from bronchitis and inflammation of the small intestine. The cold, the isolation, a lack of provisions and the slow crumbling of structure and order resulted in frequent outbreaks of illness and disease. There was not enough food or access to healthcare, be it primitive or modern.

It didn't help that members were banned from eating or drinking anything besides their set 6 p.m. meal, and that the water container they drank from during that meal was shared by everyone. There were growing concerns that followers were denied leave to return to their old lives or attempt to reintegrate into society. An eco-cult had been born and the group was dubbed a "green feather show".

As 1993 arrived, Pulliainen, the zoology professor who had once supported the Iriadamant, denounced its practices, stopped funding the group and stated that no research of value was being conducted at Kittilä. Maltais himself did not, it transpired, even live at the compound and was usually to be found in a Helsinki hotel. Worse still, reports then circulated that, on top of the already dire conditions at the camp, children were being abused.

Once the calls against it grew louder, a Finnish MP raised questions about the future of the group within the nation and requested that any further similar studies be denied. The interior minister, however, claimed that there was no obvious crime being committed by the group, and so no action was required. In the summer of 1993, the Iriadamant travelled far and wide across the country in what became known as a "Walking Speech". They painted black crosses on their faces and asked civilians to sign a petition supporting the group; this was later sent to the president, Mauno Koivisto. Despite these calls to remain, the interior minister eventually decided not to extend the residence permit of the Iriadamant, and the group was set to be deported.

By this point, the Iriadamant was regarded as a terrorist group, and 25 officers were dispatched to surround the compound. Many members were handcuffed and taken away and their passports confiscated. No charges were filed, but the Iriadamants were now effectively homeless.

There were just 56 members remaining by this stage, and, while they were booked to fly out of Finland in November 1993, they did not arrive at the airport and instead crossed the border into Sweden before heading south to the Netherlands.

In the meantime, their charismatic leader Maltais had been charged by a Belgian court with fraud and embezzlement; he was also thought to be connected to drug smuggling gangs, planned acts of terrorism and the illegal weapons trade. On the run, he fled to Nicaragua, where it is believed he died in 2015. It is assumed that once his emaciated, exhausted followers reached Italy – either on foot or in a truck – they realized all was lost and that their great leader had deserted them. The experiment was over, and the group was disbanded.

STATE WITHIN A STATE

Paul Schäfer was born in 1921 in Troisdorf, western Germany, near the border with the Netherlands. As was common for children at the time, he joined the Hitler Youth movement as a boy, and came of age just as World War Two erupted across Europe.

He did not have a particularly illustrious academic career and sustained a facial injury as a child that left him with a glass eye. During the war, it was this latter fact that left him unable to join the SS corps, and he served instead as a medic for the German army in occupied France. When 1945 arrived and Germany surrendered to the Allied forces, Schäfer decided to become a pastor in the Christian Baptist Church.

For a brief period he worked as a youth minister, but was soon asked to leave. Apparently there were concerns over his treatment of boys in his care, but it seems no direct action was taken or any crime reported. Schäfer, dressed in the traditional German costume of lederhosen, left the local area and set off into the German countryside with a guitar. Whenever he came across fellow travellers, Schäfer explained that he was a Christian minister and encouraged them to confess their sins to him. Many did, quite willingly. He was immediately trusted and attracted confidants.

Throughout the 1950s, Schäfer steadily expanded a base of followers, many of whom were widows whose husbands had been killed during the war and who had young children. He was a credible figure and his growing congregation of followers paid over 10 per cent of their earnings to him each month. However, when two of these parents accused Schäfer of molesting their children in 1959, a warrant for his arrest was issued and Schäfer fled the country.

Though it is unknown exactly how he travelled there, his next port of call was the Middle East; as many of his followers came with him from Germany, it is possible they helped finance the crossing. He eventually settled in Chile in 1961 on a settlement 4 hours south of Santiago and which comprised some 50 square miles of land. High above, reaching into the sky, were the snow-capped summits of the imposing Andes Mountains.

The purchase of the arable farming land, used for wheat, corn and soybean, cemented Schäfer's feeling that this would be a permanent arrangement where he could continue to escape justice. The plot of land was purchased with money from his group, with 230 members joining him in Chile, and was called Colonia Dignidad (Dignity Colony).

Schäfer continued to use his charm and position as a minister to encourage more and more followers to join the commune. It was viewed positively by locals as a centre of German refinement and sustainability; a place where people had a simpler life and lived off the land. It also provided the perfect escape for many Nazi leaders who were fleeing the war courts being established across Europe to try generals and soldiers for their crimes.

All members were expected to give a percentage of their earnings to Schäfer himself, or even contribute the entirety of their retirement pot to the man. Schäfer ruled over the colony with the title "eternal uncle", stating that his members' old ties were gone and that from now on they would live as one large and interconnected family. He prevented married couples from living together or engaging in any form of intercourse. Children were always segregated by sex and lived separately from their parents.

In 1966, a man called Wolfgang Müller managed to escape the colony – no mean feat, given its intensely high security – and went to the police. He stated he had joined Colonia Dignidad at the age of 16, had worked as a slave labourer, received multiple beatings during his time there and was molested by Schäfer. Following his escape, Müller became a German citizen and was instrumental in activist work against the cult that had detained him. Later, he even founded a charity designed to support other victims of Colonia Dignidad.

By the 1970s, Schäfer's community had grown steadily larger, and he was influential within the higher social circles of Chile. Since many of Schäfer's messages held anti-communist overtones it wasn't long before he began to develop a friendship with the notorious General Augusto Pinochet, the president of the country, who later became regarded as a violent and abusive tyrant responsible for many human rights crimes through the course of his reign. As the pair's friendship deepened, Schäfer offered Pinochet an attractive proposition: the president could, if he wanted, use Schäfer's colony as a detention camp for those who opposed Pinochet's regime.

Pinochet's new secret police force was established in September 1973, and from that time did its very best to find, arrest and wipe out perceived enemies of the state, dissidents and protestors. Almost 40,000 Chileans were imprisoned and 2,000 murdered.

With this many political dissidents, the use of Colonia Dignidad would prove instrumental in securing an isolated space in which to torture people or execute them en masse.

Meanwhile, followers of Schäfer quickly realized the utopian life vision they had been promised in Chile was far from the reality. Men were required to dress in woollen pants, women in home-made dresses and headscarves: this was the traditional wear of the German peasantry in times gone by. Men and women worked 16 hours a day in the fields, seven days a week. Any form of entertainment such as television, and any means of contacting outsiders or keeping time, such as telephones or calendars, was forbidden.

As the years went by, Colonia Dignidad amassed a sizeable income from selling some of its produce, including bread, vegetables and dairy products. Since it was classed a non-profit organization, this income was also exempt from tax.

From the beginning, Schäfer fostered an atmosphere of paranoia amid his supporters, who were expected to write down the names of sinners on a blackboard at every lunch and dinner. When Schäfer read out the names, the accused were forced to stand and confess – even though what they were confessing was usually entirely fabricated, they knew they had to say something. Any trouble or strife in the community led to terrible punishment and torture. Members were members for life, and leaving was absolutely forbidden – presumably, in part, to prevent any word of the hideous things that happened from reaching the wider world.

The segregation of adults by sex was also extended to children, who were cared for by nurses in the community. This enabled Schäfer to commence a years-long spree of sexual abuse, molestation, assault and rape against the male children of the commune. He would ask his inner circle to send him a boy each evening, and it is estimated that he and others abused more than 30,000 children during the commune's existence. Many were under the age of ten years old. It was claimed afterwards that some of Schäfer's terrorizing activities included, at Christmas, pretending to shoot a member who was dressed as Santa Claus. This was just one instance of his ability to instil fear and foster blind obedience among the very youngest members of the cult.

At the same time, the colony's doctors were also tasked with torturing young women. Schäfer stated that girls could not control their libido once they hit puberty and so he instructed his medics to deliver electric shocks to the genitalia, which often resulted in sterilization.

Amnesty International requested that the West German government attempt to investigate what was happening at the settlements, and publications like the *Washington Post* sent their reporters. One, Charles A. Krause, arrived at Colonia Dignidad in 1980 but was chased away by the armed guards patrolling the perimeter. This remote farm was now a highly secure, seemingly impenetrable fort complete with surveillance towers, watchdogs, electric fences and cameras.

Many members did try to escape, but if the Chilean police – who were friends of Schäfer – caught the runaways, they would simply be immediately returned to the settlement. Even when they managed to reach Chile's German embassy and explained what was happening to them, they were still returned. Deserters were usually drugged and tortured afterwards, with one man being subjected to daily electric shocks.

By the 1980s, the Colonia Dignidad had experienced a reduction in its numbers. Some older followers had died, others had mysteriously disappeared. Many women were, of course, now unable to bear children; more to the point, sex was forbidden. At this point, Schäfer opened the doors of the colony to Chilean locals. This was greeted favourably by the local population, who regarded the invitation as a privilege and an honour. Many were quite happy to send their children off to Schäfer's care, believing they would be privy to a higher standard of education and respectability in the German's orbit.

From 1990, the brutal regime of Pinochet began to crumble and a new democratic president, Patricio Aylwin, was elected. Aylwin, possibly attempting to curtail the cult's activities, charged its leader with tax evasion and removed its status as a non-profit organization. Feeling the net tightening on his decades of control and human rights abuses, Schäfer disappeared from Colonia Dignidad in the late 1990s. This enabled the escape of many members, with some going to the police. Chilean officers attended the compound and found a cache of illegal weapons, as well as secret tunnels.

By 1996, there was enough evidence for prosecutors to charge Schäfer on child abuse allegations. He remained underground and on the run for a further nine years until he was located by the journalist Carola Fuentes in 2005. Having received a tip-off, Fuentes discovered Schäfer on a ranch in Argentina, and he was arrested by local police, along with a number of accomplices. The group was extradited to Chile and received sentences in prison for a host of charges including the harbouring of firearms, murder and torture. Schäfer was indicted with sexual abuse against 25 children, though it is possible the true number of victims was considerably higher. Just five years after his 20-year sentence began, Schäfer died in prison.

The colony remains operational to this day, with some original members still living there. It has, however, changed its name to Villa Baviera and has opened a tourist retreat and a shop selling German food and beer. Some ex-members filed civil cases against the governments of both Germany and Chile, claiming that their home states did little to prevent Schäfer's abuses. Neither took responsibility initially, with the Chilean government stating the colony was "a state within a state".

Then, in 2017, the German government established a fund to compensate former members of the colony, many of whom had not contributed to pension pots for years and were then living in poverty. Germany and Chile subsequently signed an agreement to collaborate on an investigation into Colonia Dignidad and create a memorial for its many, many victims.

DESTRUCTIVE
CULTS

In this book, we've already seen just how appalling the destruction perpetrated in the name of cult ideology can be. What, then, defines a destructive cult? On the surface, followers of cults we might term "destructive" may adhere to the same principles as other categories of cult; members may live in specific communities and separate themselves from society at large. What divides these types of cult, however, is their propensity for "revolutionary" acts designed to cause damage, disruption and even death right from the outset. It will cause harm either to its own members, or to the wider population – and sometimes both.

This is nothing new. In 48 CE, a group calling themselves "the Zealots" began a campaign of terror across the Roman province of Judea. Their aim was to incite insurrection against the Romans, and the Sicarii, men carrying daggers, gained access to key Roman cities to stab legionaries or collaborators with the Roman regime. They did not limit themselves to knives and used poison against their enemies, as well as kidnapping members of the Temple

Guard. In 72 CE, the Roman general Flavius Silva attacked the Zealots' stronghold in Masada; the group's leader encouraged his members to take their own lives to avoid capture. This wanton, manic violence suggests a deeper level of psychological attachment that other cults, whose members are encouraged to be passive, do not always cultivate.

Achieving harm doesn't always constitute mere physical acts of violence, but can of course extend to psychological abuse. In this respect, many of the stories described in this book can be termed as such: tales in which followers are persuaded into dependency on the cult or its leader, become dehumanized over time, understand that they possess no legal rights and commit to membership for life. Most importantly of all, members are usually brainwashed into rejecting any authority but that of their leader; this, in turn, emboldens them with the ability to commit some of the atrocities discussed in the pages that follow.

BRANCHING OUT

In 1955, an American named Benjamin Roden, then 53 years old, set up what was described as a continuation of the Seventh-day Adventist Church. Roden had converted from Judaism to Christianity around the time of his marriage in 1937. The General Association of Davidian Seventh-day Adventists had been established by the Bulgarian Victor Houteff, and was focused on reformation of the original Church's teachings. As these were rejected by the traditional arm of the Seventh-day Adventists, Houteff and his followers moved in 1935 to an area of land outside Waco in Texas. Roden is thought to have joined in 1940.

After Houteff's death in 1955, Roden declared he had received a fresh message from God. He wrote a series of letters, all signed from "the Branch", and suggested this was the new name taken by Jesus Christ. When people started listening, they joined the new offshoot of Houteff's sect and became the Branch Davidians.

One of the cult's followers was Vernon Wayne Howell. His had not been a happy upbringing: he'd been born to a 14-year-old single mother, herself a Seventh-day Adventist, whose subsequent boyfriend was described as a violent alcoholic. Howell lived for a brief spell with his maternal grandmother before returning to his mother at the age of seven. A lonely, isolated child who suffered bullying at school, he was placed in the special educational unit at school and dropped out of high school in his junior year. At the age of 19, he had sex with an underage teenager and this resulted in her pregnancy. Howell joined the Southern Baptist Church but was soon expelled for having told the pastor that God wanted him to take the man's 12-year-old daughter as his wife.

By 1977, Howell went by a new name, David Koresh, and in 1981 he arrived in Waco and joined the Davidians in earnest. He was known to have played the guitar at the group's centre at Mount Carmel, where he also sang during services. When Benjamin Roden died in 1979, his wife Lois assumed the leadership of the Davidians. Lois Roden was a popular leader; she was vocal in her support of the feminist movement, was a known TV star and evangelizer, and was seemingly widely liked by her many followers.

For the first two years after his arrival, David Koresh was her polar opposite. Most followers found him haughty and pompous, and Lois Roden asked Koresh to live apart from the others in a much smaller, unfurnished room. In 1983, Koresh came to Lois with a startling revelation. He claimed that God had told him he was to father "the chosen one", and that Lois was to be the child's mother. However, Lois already had a son, George, who was expected to take the helm at the Davidians upon his mother's death. George was soon informed of Koresh's wild claims and attempted to have him expelled from the Mount Carmel headquarters. This proved unsuccessful as it is believed Lois thought she was indeed pregnant by this point with Koresh's child.

Koresh then changed tack and announced instead that he had been called to marry another young member of the group, 14-year-old Rachel Jones. He then collected a group of 25 followers and set out for the "wilderness", founding yet another splinter group in Palestine, Texas, about 100 miles east of Waco. He left the group behind soon after and began recruitment missions abroad, notably to Israel and Australia.

Followers flocked to Koresh over the subsequent years. The daughters of new disciples who joined the Davidians sect usually became Koresh's wives. He was known to have a distinctive, mesmerizing oratorical style, and could recite whole verses of scripture from memory. Soon enough he was claiming to be the world's final prophet. His key message was that the end of the world was nigh and would take place when he converted the Jewish population of Israel to his own cause. When this took place, the United States would invade the Holy Land and this, he said, would commence Armageddon, or the apocalypse. This prophecy would later prove untrue when he travelled to Israel, and he then claimed instead that the battle between his own followers and the US army would take place in Texas.

The original Waco compound found itself with heavy debts to pay some years later when Lois Roden died. This presented Koresh with an opportunity and he raised the money to buy the Mount Carmel headquarters, bringing his own supporters from Palestine with him and merging the two groups. There were now around 100 members residing on the compound and under Koresh's leadership some drastic changes were implemented: notably a bus, buried underground, which was to serve as a bunker when the apocalypse came. Koresh was known to separate married couples and invited women followers to join him each night for "Bible study".

Meanwhile, the early 1990s saw the Federal Bureau of Investigation (FBI) beginning their own enquiries into Koresh's practices, as ex-members had come forward with stories of polygamy, accusations of child abuse and the harbouring of illegal weapons.

On 28 February 1993, at 4.20 a.m., employees of the Bureau of Alcohol, Tobacco, Firearms and Explosives (ATF) arrived at the compound with a warrant. It was a Sunday, deliberately planned so as not to cause alarm to the group's members who, it was assumed, would be at church. What they didn't know was that the Davidians observed the Sabbath on Saturday.

When the ATF arrived, it attempted to gain entry to the heavily fortified compound. They were searching Mount Carmel for machine guns, and for the first 45 minutes the ATF attempted to shoot its way inside, and then the bullets ran out. During this first period of the siege, on 28 February, four agents of the government organization were killed, and 16 wounded. Five members of the cult also died. The ATF tried to establish a dialogue with Koresh, and the FBI took command and oversaw the release of 19 children from the compound over the following weeks. When these children were interviewed, many described experiencing physical and sexual abuse inside the walls of Mount Carmel. The Bureau's worst fears were being confirmed in real time, and yet they were no closer to capturing Koresh. Officials could never have anticipated that their arrival would result in a siege lasting over 50 days.

For the next six weeks, a violent battle took place across the compound. Each evening, a rapt American audience would tune in to the news, horrified at the scenes of devastation and death playing out across their screens.

On 19 April 1993, the FBI pushed once more to gain entry, this time using 12.7 mm rifles, armoured tanks and tear gas. Fires were started, it was believed deliberately, inside the headquarters. Buildings collapsed, smoke billowed out and guns were systematically loaded, emptied and reloaded. With the aid of a battering ram, law enforcement finally managed to enter the compound. Meanwhile, 79 Davidians had died in the fires, of whom 21 were children. One three-year-old had been stabbed in the chest.

The exact nature of Koresh's death is unknown, but he was confirmed to have died on 19 April from a gunshot wound to the head. A congressional hearing later took place, aiming to understand the nature of law enforcement activity during the siege, and civil suits were brought against the US government and federal officials. During this inquiry, President Bill Clinton condemned Koresh's "depravity", stating that there was "no moral equivalency between the disgusting acts which took place inside that compound in Waco and the efforts that law enforcement officers made to enforce the law and protect innocent people".

To this day, there are numerous groups in existence that purport to descend from the Branch Davidians. One group of the same name claimed that Lois Roden's true successor was Doug Mitchell, a member since 1978 who died in 2013. They have rejected ever having followed Koresh.

The event came to be known as the Waco siege and represented the largest gunfight in US history after the Civil War. In 1995, the two men responsible for the Oklahoma City bombing, Timothy McVeigh and Terry Nichols, which took place on the second anniversary of the siege's bloody end, stated that they had planned the attack to coincide with the date in question.

FROM MOURNING TO REJOICING

The Cult of the Dead was an eerily named group that fully lived up to its billing. This group was formed through the legend of the ancient Egyptian corn god, Osiris. The son of Geb and Nut, Osiris was purportedly born in Thebes in northern Egypt. He was heir to the throne and, when he took the role, he also took his sister, Isis, as his queen consort. He taught his followers to farm, abolished cannibalism and was known as "the good one".

The ancient Egyptians believed that the god's brother, Set, attempted to assassinate Osiris: he held a banquet and produced a beautiful coffin, claiming that it would be given to whomever it fitted best. When Osiris climbed inside, Set closed the lid before dumping the box in the Nile. Isis, stricken with grief, attempted to locate her husband and eventually found the coffin before returning it to Egypt, where she hid it. Set discovered the ruse and removed Osiris' body, which he hacked into 14 separate parts, before throwing them all in the river. Isis gathered the body parts, bandaged the corpse and produced the first mummy. At this point, Osiris travelled to the underworld to judge and rule over the spirits of the dead.

Evidence of followers of Osiris are found from the twenty-fifth century BCE: he was depicted as green skinned, with a beard, wearing a crown of feathers and holding a crook. Iconography featuring the god was widespread, as were temples, statues and models.

It is thought that followers of the Cult of the Dead were particularly moved by the notion that a violent death might not necessitate a violent afterlife, and that rebirth and reincarnation were possible. The legend of Osiris symbolizes destruction and reunification, good over evil. According to the story, after Osiris' body was restored he and Isis were able to conceive their son, Horus, who went on to rival the jealous brother Set, who now sat on the throne. Throughout many violent escapades, Horus the sun god emerged triumphant and was said to have restored order to Egypt. The line of succession, so brutally destroyed through murder, had been restored.

The myth of Osiris was incorporated into many Egyptian texts and was often recounted at funerals. Parents told their rapt children the tale and accounts survive of spells cast in honour of Osiris, whose conception of a child after death represented a new and fascinating kind of magic. The cult of Osiris was unusual in that, prior to its inception, promises of the afterlife were ordinarily the preserve of the ruling classes. For believers of Osiris and observers of the cult, however, hierarchy was unimportant, and everyone would enjoy eternal life through him.

Over time, the legend developed to position Osiris as the god of nature, seasonal rebirth in spring and the annual flooding of the River Nile.

Every November, a mystery festival took place to mark the death of Osiris. An image of the god would be paraded through town and venerated by the public and worshippers. This would be followed by a drama depicting the murder and dismemberment of Osiris and the search for his body. Each year, it was hoped that these acts would bring more followers to the cause and grow the cult further still.

Julius Firmicus Maternus, a Roman writer and astrologer, described the worshippers who: "beat their breasts and gnashed their shoulders... when they pretend that the mutilated remains of the god have been found and rejoined... they turn from mourning to rejoicing."

As general adoration of Osiris grew, the acts of worship associated with the cults became ever darker. There is evidence that slaves were slaughtered at the graves of members of the monarchy and other nobles: this was intended to ward off evil spirits. Gruesomely, human heads were discovered in the tombs of Osiris, suggesting that homage to the god was not limited to songs, stories and iconography. The Greek philosopher Plutarch described these sacrifices, unsurprisingly, as "gloomy, solemn and mournful".

These "retainer sacrifices" – when servants were killed and buried, or "retained", alongside their masters – were believed to raise the status of the nobility and were often enacted after the death of a pharaoh. It was believed that the nobility's slaves would join them in the afterlife and they would thus be regarded more favourably by Osiris. If a nobleman was buried along with all his treasure and possessions, including his slaves, he was seen as more powerful, especially if he was buried close to the pharaoh. The idea that the afterlife would bring about eternal joy and security was the motivating force behind such sacrifices.

The Cult of the Dead was practised primarily in ancient Egypt, sometime from the fourth century BCE, particularly on the upper banks of the Nile, at Abydos and Dendera. A huge cult shrine was found at Abydos, built from cedar wood with segments of lapis lazuli, bronze and gold across a statue of Osiris. Believers felt that, on death, Osiris would judge them and decide if their souls were to be forever lost or whether they would pass on to the afterlife.

In the 1890s, the British Egyptologist Flinders Petrie discovered the tomb of King Aha in Abydos, one of the known sites at which the cult was understood to be prevalent. King Aha had been the second pharaoh to rule over the First Dynasty of Egypt, in which the country's upper and lower regions were united. The excavation revealed several additional graves outside the pharaoh's funeral site, with all of the remains found to be of men between the ages of 20 and 25 years old. They showed signs of strangulation. The similarities in age, sex and method of death indicated a mass human sacrifice.

Until the rise of Christianity across the Roman Empire, Osiris was worshipped far and wide and was a fixture of ancient Egyptian religious practice. It was only when the Theodosian decree was announced in 380 CE that paganism was repressed with a vengeance. Many temples dedicated to Osiris were destroyed, priests involved in the worship of the Cult of the Dead were imprisoned or killed, and sacred images featuring Osiris were taken to Constantinople. At this point, the emergence of Christianity meant the cult began to fade out of public consciousness and worship.

DON'T MESS WITH US

Ever used the phrase: "Fake it till you make it"? What about putting someone "in the hot seat"? And the less common, though still prevalent: "Today is the first day of the rest of your life"? All three of these slogans trace their origins back to Synanon, an organization originally based in Santa Monica, California, which boasts ardent followers to this day.

For a time, their outreach work was said to rival Alcoholics Anonymous' (AA) 12-step programme. Synanon was originally conceived in 1958 by Charles E. Dederich Sr as a drug rehabilitation and community support system. Dederich was himself a former member of AA, where he sometimes spoke for hours at a time without pause.

Dederich had a difficult past. His father had been an alcoholic and died in a car accident when Dederich was just four. He had been raised as a devout Roman Catholic but renounced his faith at the age of 14 after reading H. G. Wells' *The Outline of History*. He turned to drink and struggled to hold down work as an adult; he'd been married, divorced and married again. At the age of 29, he contracted meningitis, which almost killed him and led to a facial droop for the rest of his life.

Dederich arrived in Santa Monica at the age of 40 and began attending AA meetings most days. He soon volunteered for a new trial at UCLA that used LSD as a "cure" for alcoholism. He would go on to cite this as a profound epiphany, a learning experience that totally altered his outlook and character. He stopped going to AA meetings as regularly as he had previously done and was living off just $33 a week in unemployment cheques from the government.

Drug-dependent users were considered differently to those suffering from alcoholism in the 1960s. Some were turned away from AA meetings and felt there was little support available to them in comparison with those addicted to alcohol. Dederich was aware of this discrepancy and formed his own non-profit group dedicated to drug users and their support. This was called Tender Loving Care, and its first headquarters were no bigger than a small, dingy store in Ocean Park. Dederich predicted the group would become as famous as Coca-Cola, but the city inspectors deemed the building to be unsafe and had it demolished. As a result, Dederich and his 65 followers moved to the old National Guard Armory building on the Santa Monica coastline.

Dederich, who was in touch with fellow AA members, invited them to get together three times a week. He immersed himself in psychology and philosophy texts, and developed the theory that addicts were not legitimate adults and should not be treated as such. Members took to calling him "Dad". These sessions became known as "synanons": a mixture of "seminar" or "symposium", and "anonymous".

Just ten days after the fledgling group moved from the Ocean Park headquarters to the old Armory building, Dederich and three other members were arrested for treating addicts without a licence; the group's leader spent just over three weeks in prison for the offence. This did not seem to deter either

Dederich or his members, and numbers grew exponentially as the years progressed. In 1967, the Synanon group purchased a large beachside hotel, again in Santa Monica, and declared the site its new headquarters; the space also housed a dormitory for drug users during treatment. Synanon then purchased the former Athens Athletic Club buildings in Oakland, California, and this site, which had its own school, became the home of the community at large.

Synanon was not the first rehabilitation centre in the United States, but it fundamentally changed perceptions about addiction throughout the country and abroad. For the first time, it offered the chance of redemption to drug addicts and championed the idea of former addicts helping to counsel new members, a practice that exists to this day.

Following the economy's boom in the years after World War Two, the average American citizen was enjoying a higher income and more disposable wealth. This in turn, coupled with the 1960s hippie culture and free love movements, increased drug culture across the board, with young people developing addictions to marijuana and heroin in particular. Promoters of cannabis claimed that it was a harmless drug and lobbied for its social acceptance.

The idea of protecting and aiding addicts was one that appealed to the authorities, politicians and ordinary American citizens alike. Senator Thomas J. Dodd, for instance, claimed that Synanon could "lead the way in the future to an effective treatment for not only drug addicts but also criminals and juvenile delinquents". For years, addicts had been largely ignored by society: treated by medical doctors in traditional hospitals or, failing that, incarcerated for indeterminate periods of time.

In 1965, *Synanon* – a film starring Edmond O'Brien as Dederich and Eartha Kitt as Betty, Dederich's third wife, herself a recovering addict – was released. The group had achieved a national and international platform, and its reputation was largely positive. Part of the reason for this, besides its apparent ethos, was that – unlike many other organizations that have since come to be regarded as cults – Synanon was comparatively transparent to the general public. Every Saturday evening the group threw a party, complete with a jazz band, and ordinary citizens unaffiliated with Synanon were welcome to attend. They sold promotional items, like pens and other kinds of stationery, complete with the Synanon logo.

Dederich was adored by the media and many mainstream publications featured glowing reports of his methods and approach to a long-standing societal problem. "Crime is stupid, delinquency is stupid, and the use of narcotics is stupid," he was quoted as saying in the *New York Times*. "What Synanon is dealing with is addiction to stupidity." Dederich himself claimed that the success rate of addicts remaining free from drugs after the Synanon programme was 80 per cent.

By 1968, the organization claimed 1,100 members, received $2.5 million a year in donations, and owned $7 million of real estate across various cities in California, as well as in Detroit, New York City and Puerto Rico. Professional psychiatrists were invited to join the group, and some did, regardless of whether they actually had any history of drug addiction.

Prior to this point, recovering addicts could hope to "graduate" from the two-year Synanon programme. In 1969, however, the direction of travel changed. Now, the only way to ensure lifelong abstinence from addiction was to remain within the Synanon community. Dederich established a "punk squad" whose purpose was to discipline new recruits who had been sent to Synanon either by law enforcement or by their parents. In addition, Dederich announced a new type of therapy would take precedence, to be known as The Game. This innovative form of group therapy was centred around the concept of "tough love", and involved humiliation and the revelation of others' fallibilities, shortcomings and secrets. Attack therapy, as The Game might be known today, is a pseudo-therapeutic technique that encourages aggression, confrontation and public denouncements.

At the time, the United States was developing a keen interest in self-reflection, openness, honesty and addressing past traumas; this was known as the "human potential" movement, which opened avenues for cynical leaders to exploit. Alongside Synanon, cults such as the People's Temple (see page 18), the Manson Family (page 287) and Heaven's Gate (page 314) had sprouted in this time. Suddenly, Synanon was not the accepting, non-judgemental utopia it had once been, and its clientele shifted too; middle-class non-addicts began flocking to its treatment centres around the country and paying handsomely for the privilege.

In 1974, the group was renamed: it was now the Church of Synanon. The federal government granted the group religious status, which provided many tax benefits and removed its need to be licensed. Synanon was now a religion, not an organization. Of course, whatever it started as and whatever it called itself, it was now a cult: believers shaved their heads and wore nothing but overalls. Monologues were broadcast by Dederich across "the Wire", an FM radio station. Husbands and wives were separated within the community. Men were forced to have vasectomies, with 80 being performed in 1976 alone, and women were forced into terminations if they became pregnant. If members tried to refuse, the group therapy sessions would focus entirely on belittling, attacking and degrading the reluctant party until they acquiesced.

As the years progressed, so did instances of crimes committed by Synanon members. In late 1972, Rose Lena Cole, who had received a court order to attend Synanon, was never heard from again. Violence became normalized, with Dederich claiming it helped keep control, and mass beatings often involved teenagers being attacked in front of their parents.

In 1975, three members admitted to assault of a Marin County ranger, while one rancher reported being pistol-whipped by the group. So-called Synanites also badly beat two Black couples who had parked at a Synanon building. Dederich himself was untouchable when it came to attack, it seemed: the organization now had its own security forces and a paramilitary group called the Imperial Marines. They even practised their own form of martial arts, called syn-do, and had an enormous armoury full of guns, which Dederich claimed were for self-defence purposes. The cult also owned at least 200 cars, 400 motorbikes, 62 freight trucks, 20 boats and 12 planes. Imperial Marines were also tasked with preparing a list of "enemies" of Synanon. An ex-member called Phil Ritter had his skull fractured by the group, fell into a coma and almost died from bacterial meningitis.

In June 1977, a 25-year-old housewife called Frances Winn went to her local doctor and asked for a tranquilizer. She had been feeling anxious and was then referred to the Santa Monica branch of Synanon. Once she entered the building, she later stated, her head was shaved, she was placed on a bus and driven to northern California, cut off from her husband, Ed, and was held captive for nine days until Ed persuaded officials to let her go.

Paul Morantz was a lawyer who had previously worked as a journalist. He sued Synanon for its treatment of Winn, and claimed the group had abducted the young woman, tortured and brainwashed her for purposes of financial gain, taking advantage of her emotional instability. Morantz won the case for the Winn family and began a campaign of dissidence against Synanon. Soon enough he began to receive threatening phone calls, day and night; he checked his car for bombs before driving.

His fear, it seems, was well founded. Dederich railed against Morantz on his radio broadcasting, asking his followers: "Why doesn't someone break his legs?... We are not going to mess with the old-time 'turn the other cheek' religious posture. Our religious posture is, 'Don't mess with us.' You can get killed, dead, physically dead. We either have a good thing here or we don't. If we have a good thing here, then we are not going to permit people like greedy lawyers to destroy it."

On 11 October 1977, Morantz returned to his home in Pacific Palisades and prepared to watch a baseball game. He noticed a package in his mailbox and, when he opened it, he let out an ear-splitting scream: a 4½-ft-long rattlesnake emerged, opening its fangs and sinking them straight into Morantz's hand. Its rattle had even been removed so as not to alert Morantz beforehand. The news anchor Walter Cronkite, in his reportage of the incident, declared it "bizarre even by cult standards". Morantz was hospitalized for six days following the attack.

This event served as the catalyst for investigations by the Los Angeles Police Department in November 1978. Dederich was arrested at his Lake Havasu compound on suspicion of conspiracy to commit murder, and two years later he pleaded no contest to this charge. He was given a five-year probation sentence owing to ill health, ordered to pay a fine of $10,000, and Synanon itself was made liable for its first tax bill, to the tune of $17 million.

Largely based on evidence gathered by Morantz, the courts ruled against Synanon's "policy of terror and violence", and the group's members – those who had not been implicated in acts of terrorism, attempted murder and financial corruption – filtered away rapidly. It filed for bankruptcy and, in 1991 and after 43 years, it was dissolved. Dederich died in 1997 and Synanon has since been called one of the most dangerous and violent cults ever known in America.

A BLOODY COVENANT

Supremacist groups lend themselves to destruction disturbingly easily, and The Covenant, the Sword and the Arm of the Lord (CSA) is just one case in point. This white supremacist group was founded in Arkansas in 1970 and its founder was the Texan minister James Ellison, whose survivalist Christian group was, at first, called Zarephath-Horeb. The sect's name stemmed from biblical readings in which God ordered Elijah to move to the city of Zarephath, where he would undergo a test of his faith.

Like many cult leaders, Ellison preached primarily about the apocalypse. In 1976, he purchased a 224-acre farm around two miles from the town of Oakland in Missouri, and the new tribe named the site Mount Horeb. This was the name of the mountain to which Moses brought the Hebrews after their flight from Egypt. Ellison had chosen the area specifically due to its demographics: most residents in that area were white and it was sufficiently isolated to discourage police from frequent visits. The site had its own water supply and was soon generating its own power: entirely self-sufficient and entirely cut off. Members were encouraged to steal what they needed from department stores, such as provisions, clothes and food, acts that meant the group attracted criticism and negative attention from its inception.

The Covenant, the Sword and the Arm of the Lord supported the fledgling American Christian Patriot Movement, and were ardent advocates of an increasingly popular notion, prevalent during that time, that the United States required racial and religious "purification". They believed that Jewish populations and non-white communities were the spawn of Satan, and they were also advocates of freedom from governmental authority above county level.

Despite being a fundamentalist minister prior to the group's creation, Ellison had previously spent time in prison, where he had published a newsletter promoting his supremacist views. He was "mentored" by other high-ranking members of extreme right-wing groups and was closely linked to the Ku Klux Klan (see page 133). He believed that God had directed him to establish a refuge and asked that ex-convicts and drug addicts join him in this mission to create a new, isolated community.

Until 1979, however, racism was not necessarily an overt component of the cult. At this point, Ellison adopted the white-supremacist theology of Christian Identity. The roots of this were founded in seventeenth-century America, when Puritan followers saw themselves as the "New Israel" and believed they were responsible for bringing about God's true intentions for humanity.

The group began to undertake paramilitary training at the compound; other organizations with the same beliefs, such as Aryan Nations, the Militia of Montana and The Order, also attended training at the cult's Endtime Overcomer Survival Training School. Here, followers were taught wilderness survival and how to practise urban warfare. It was at this point that the group's name was changed from Zarephath-Horeb Community Church to The Covenant, the Sword and the Arm of the Lord. The compound now boasted firing ranges and huge armouries full of guns. The site would now be regarded, Ellison said, as an "ark for God's people" when the "race war" finally erupted. The war, he claimed, would bring about the country's economic collapse and his followers needed to be prepared for the famine, rioting and bloodshed that would inevitably follow.

The compound was positioned at the crossover points of the states of Missouri and Arkansas and this, Ellison hoped, would further complicate any legal issues he might need to contend with later. If the jurisdiction of his compound was in any way disputed, this made life easier for the cult leader. Ellison and his tribe believed that Jewish leaders were overly influential when it came to the media and financial positions of power in the country, and that they were determined to see the collapse of the federal government. He encouraged his members to grow their own food and to stockpile weapons across their huge headquarters.

Despite the intensity and scale of the CSA's preparations, the FBI estimated in 1982 that the group comprised just 100 members. The problem was that those members were becoming increasingly militarized and radical in their approach to spreading the views originally espoused by Ellison. Over time, the CSA became a major weapons distributor and disseminated hate literature; it also sold silencers and explosives at gun shows, which in turn became its primary recruitment ground.

A supremacist meeting was held in the summer of 1983, which various groups, including the CSA, attended. They put together a manifesto whose aim was the overthrow of the US's so-called "Zionist-Occupied" government. They intended to create a new Aryan nation, and a computer system that would enable the groups to communicate was also discussed. The groups' combined strategy involved the murder of government officials and Jewish communities, the destruction of public amenities such as water systems and the bombing of federal buildings. These terrorist acts would, they hoped, precipitate a revolution and enable the white-power groups to take hold.

During that same year of 1983, a white supremacist named Gordon Kahl was killed in a federal raid; he had previously shot dead two US marshals months prior. Kahl, who was from North Dakota, became an idealized figure to the CSA and they began to plan for the assassination of any officials who had presided over Kahl's prosecution for murder. These targets included an FBI agent, a US attorney and a judge.

The murders were never carried out, but 1983 represented the commencement of the cult's major criminal activities. At the end of that year, they were responsible for arson attacks at an Arkansas church with a large homosexual congregation, and a firebombing at a synagogue in Indiana. They also tried to bomb a natural gas pipeline in Chicago, one that supplied much of mid-western America. In the same month, they also detonated explosives on an electrical-transmission line at Fort Smith in Arkansas.

The following day, having been unsuccessful in this attempt, one member of the group murdered a pawnshop owner in Arkansas, whom he believed to be Jewish. The same man, Richard Wayne Snell, went on in 1984 to kill a Black state trooper called Louis Bryant. Snell had been stopped by Bryant for a traffic-related incident, but pulled his gun and fired. He was arrested and was executed by lethal injection on 19 April 1995, just 12 hours after the Oklahoma City bombings. Of course, 19 April was a key date during which the siege at Waco, Texas, took place amid the federal government's sting operation against the Branch Davidians (see page 177).

On that very same day, over 300 FBI agents, along with other members of the US police forces, surrounded the CSA compound. They had been working with informants who provided details of alleged crimes there, including the murder of a woman, and the group's huge hoard of weapons, booby traps around the site and its training techniques. Local residents had long complained about the CSA's activities, and it was thought that a member of The Order, David Tate, was currently or would soon be arriving at the site; he was wanted for the murder of a state trooper.

For the next four days, the two sides battled across the walls of the CSA's headquarters. Multiple weapons were seized, as was ammunition, explosives, gold and, most shockingly, some 30 gallons of potassium cyanide. It was believed that the poison was intended to be introduced to the water supply of large cities.

A member of the group emerged on the fourth day and began to negotiate with the agents. He reported back to Ellison that the FBI were willing to accept his surrender and that they would empty the site on entry. When Ellison himself emerged for negotiations, the agents convinced him that, if an armed fight did occur, the CSA was very likely to lose. Ellison's spiritual adviser, Robert G. Millar, was even flown to the headquarters to help persuade Ellison that enough was enough. Deciding not to risk his members, or indeed himself, falling victim to FBI gunfire, Ellison surrendered on 22 April 1985.

Later that year, he was charged with attempting to overthrow the US government – though these charges were later dropped – and eventually sentenced to 20 years in prison on charges of harbouring illegal weapons and racketeering. Through the course of its activities, the CSA was suspected of counterfeiting, arson, robbery, murder and plotting acts of terrorism. Ellison was able to reduce this sentence, nonetheless, by testifying against other leaders of the Aryan Nations group. He was released from prison in 1987. Since that time, the CSA is believed to have disbanded: a cult reliant on and driven by one fanatical leader.

CLAWS AND TEETH

In 1888, a British colonial official published a book describing his experience of what was then known as the Colony and Protectorate of Sierra Leone. The country was under British administration from 1808 until 1961, when it achieved its independence.

The book, written by George Alexander Lethbridge Banbury, described the high mortality rates of colonialists, whether from tropical diseases like malaria or other sicknesses relating to climate or sanitation standards. Banbury was himself sent back to Britain after he contracted malaria. The book intensified widespread fear and mistrust of the African colonies at the time, particularly given its title: *Sierra Leone; or, the White Man's Grave*. But it was Banbury's description of one particular cult group that stoked the most revulsion and terror.

The Leopard Society was active at the time Banbury lived and worked in Sierra Leone. A secret society, its members were believed to possess the power to transform into leopards by using witchcraft. The group's influence, possibly fuelled by the fear they instilled in people, spread from its country of origin to Liberia and the Ivory Coast, but it was particularly prominent among the Efik ethnic group, which could be found in southern Nigeria and western Cameroon. By the 1840s, the practice had spread to other countries in southern and eastern Africa.

The cult was all male and is known to be one of the oldest in African history. Initially, it was established as a method of self-defence, with the aim of protecting people from night-time raids by rival groups or communities. It enabled alliances during times of war and was initially thought to improve trade relations and collect debts.

By the 1800s, however, its practices had grown altogether grislier. At the time, the colonial authorities were determined to establish dominance over their regions and stamp out societies such as the Leopards, which were deemed primitive and barbaric. Furthermore, the military strength of the colonialists, in addition to their organization, training and sheer numbers, far surpassed those of the Indigenous secret societies, who had once dealt with local matters of policing in their own way. As time went on and the colonialists' presence intensified, these societies began to feel their power slipping away.

Their tactics were horribly violent: the men usually travelled in packs of four or six, and dressed in leopard skins, lying in wait for travellers and biding their time. When their prey approached, they used sharp knives that looked like claws and teeth to apprehend the helpless victims. Their bodies would be torn open, their blood drained and their flesh cut away. The group would then gorge on the body and would gift certain portions, such as skin or organs, to other members of the cult to eat.

In the *Journal of the Society of Comparative Legislation*, dating back to the decade between 1896 and 1906, British officials updated their legislation in the following manner:

> *Whereas there exists in the Imperi country a society known by the name of the Human Leopard Society, formed for the purpose of committing murder, and*

where many murders have been committed by men dressed so as to represent leopards, and armed with a three-pronged knife, commonly known as a leopard-knife, or other weapon.

From 1895, therefore, anyone wearing leopard skins or found in possession of the cult's trademark knives, without good reason, was to be found guilty of felony, with a maximum prison sentence of 14 years.

Their victims were often Westerners or slave dealers who would traditionally ambush such tribes at night: the Leopard Society was mostly nocturnal as a result. However, the group achieved near-mythical levels of societal dread because it was indiscriminate – if a native man or woman happened to pass while they were waiting, they too were attacked. At the end of December 1912, a girl of seven was killed in Nerekoro in what was first believed to have been an attack by a bush leopard. Two days later, however, a girl of 12 was also killed, and another of the same age the month following. Witnesses later came forward to describe the dreadful sight not of dangerous beasts attacking the children, but members of the Leopard Society.

They became known across the country as "Mforoekpe", a name that soon became synonymous with bloodshed and cannibalism. Members were known as "Leopard Men", the leopard being a symbol of power and strength for many West African tribes. Many followers lived across the towns of Sherbro Island in Sierra Leon; its many rivers and mangrove creeks were the perfect hiding places. These were seldom visited by outsiders for any legitimate purpose and its inhabitants knew them far better than any outsider. The rivers also provided an isolated escape route, often undertaken on canoes once the murders had been committed.

It was unclear to the outside world exactly what motivated the Leopard Society to commit such acts of cannibalism. One theory is that the cult believed that human flesh provided them with the strength they required. Blood and organs were thought to pacify evil spirits and cure diseases, but also protect the consumer from poverty. Another theory was that human body parts were added to a medicine bag or *borfina*, with skin and blood believed to enrich the healing properties of the bag and its contents. The practice could also have developed from a religious ritual into an acquired appetite for human flesh. Another possibility is that the ingestion of human flesh was regarded as an act of loyalty to the cult, a marker of community and allegiance to the secret society.

New members were often lost wanderers, either local or foreign, who happened to come across the Leopards. They were then given a stark choice, if they were male: either be killed immediately or initiated into the cult. If he agreed to join, a small cut would enable some of his blood to be given to the *borfina*, during which time he was not permitted to make any sign or show any pain. The "Master" of the group would cut a small piece of flesh from his left buttock, his blood would be taken as "tribute" and he would be required to swear an oath never to reveal the secrets of the Leopard Society. Soon enough, his initiation would be complete by the witness of, or partaking in, the cult's next murder and the consumption of the victim's flesh.

The so-called sister branch of the Leopards was the Crocodile Society, which in time was joined by the Baboon Society, both of which also practised cannibalism. In 1930, a German doctor called Werner Junge travelled to Liberia, where he intended to establish a hospital in the heart of the jungle. He went on to describe many encounters with both the Leopard and Crocodile Societies, and witnessed the aftermath of the groups' ritualistic murders, or attempted murders:

There, on a mat in a house, I found the horribly mutilated body of a fifteen-year-old girl. The neck was torn to ribbons by the teeth and claws of the animal, the intestines were torn out, the pelvis shattered, and one thigh was missing. A part of the thigh, gnawed to the bone, and a piece of the shin-bone lay near the body.

Junge thought at first that a beast of prey had committed the attack, but an examination of the meticulous wounds and regular cuts left him in no doubt that humans were actually responsible.

One scholar at the time remarked that human fat was thought to have "replenished the energy of some primitive entity". The modern writer Stephen Ellis wrote of the Leopards as "exclusive groups of people who were believed to be liable to possession by the spirits of carnivorous animals such as leopards and crocodiles, and who carried out ritual killings while in a state of possession".

The groups were notoriously difficult to apprehend, but the countries involved and their police forces mounted an effort to do so during the twentieth century. The Liberian government condemned the Leopards as outlaws during this time and local courts were set up specifically to handle crimes of this nature. In one account of authorities' attempts to curtail the Leopard Society's crimes, a trap was created for a group based in Gabon, which resulted in a member of the cult being shot dead while eating his victim. Several members of the Society were caught and some were hanged. As the century progressed, fewer and fewer instances of the cult's bloody activities were recorded until it was thought to have died out altogether.

LOS NARCOSATÁNICOS

In 1962, a teenage Cuban immigrant named Delia Aurora González gave birth to a son in Miami and named him Adolfo Constanzo. She went on to have three other children and marry, when she moved to San Juan in Puerto Rico. Delia, along with her own mother, practised Santeria, a religion that developed in Cuba in the late nineteenth century and combines elements of the West African Yoruba religion, Catholicism and spiritism. Indeed, she and her mother were considered "Santeras", or high priestesses within the faith.

During his childhood, Constanzo was a member of the Catholic Church and served as an altar boy. However, he also visited Haiti with his mother, and it was here that he learned about the ancient practice of vodou. He would have learned about different deities during this time and how to make offerings to them. He was also expelled from his elementary school as a young boy, though exactly why is not known.

At the age of ten, Constanzo and his family returned to the United States, and the death of his stepfather led to a further decrease in the family's already low income. Adolfo was purportedly apprenticed to a sorcerer in Miami during his adolescence – though it is unclear how the pair met – and started to practise Palo Mayombe, which came from the Congo

Basin and which also developed in Cuba at the same time as Santeria.

Primary to the Palo belief system is the deity Nsambi, or Sambia, who is understood as the creator of the earth's first man and woman, and, although prayers are not offered up to Nsambi directly, animal sacrifice is a component of worship. Constanzo's new stepfather, following his mother's remarriage, was a drug dealer who also practised Palo Mayombe. If any local confrontation occurred, neighbours of the family soon began to complain of dead animals being left outside their doors.

Both Constanzo and his mother were arrested throughout his youth, usually on charges of theft and shoplifting, but also vandalism. When he graduated from high school, Constanzo took work briefly as a male model and relocated to Mexico City, where he met Martín Quintana, Jorge Montes and Omar Orea. Together the four men established a magic business, which involved displays of animal sacrifice. These spells were popular among ordinary citizens and rich society alike and were believed to bring good luck. He was soon mixing with the city's infamous drug cartels, who believed Constanzo capable of providing protection during smuggling operations.

In the Palo belief system, the consecrated bones of animals are held in a ceremonial cauldron called a *nganga*. As a young man, Constanzo decided that the local graveyard provided the best opportunity for procuring bones to place inside the cauldron. This soon escalated, however, when he and his followers decided that the spirits of the dead within the pot would be stronger if live humans were offered as the sacrifice instead of the bones of long-dead bodies.

As Constanzo's popularity and the number of his followers grew, the emerging cult leader attempted to go into business partnership with the Calzadas, one of the city's major drug-running families. The family declined. Soon after, seven of its members disappeared in mysterious circumstances, and their corpses were later discovered with missing fingers, toes, ears and brains. Constanzo's next acquaintance with a drug-running family went altogether more smoothly as he developed connections with the Hernandez family, who had large numbers of relatives on both sides of the United States and Mexico border. They were known to smuggle a ton of marijuana a week, and the family's president, Elio, believed ardently in Constanzo's supposed powers of supernatural ministry. Constanzo, along with his followers, now moved to the Rancho Santa Elena: a lonely house in Matamoros, Mexico, surrounded by desert and owned by the Hernandez family. There, he stored his vast amounts of cocaine and marijuana. Over the months and years that followed, more and more members of the Hernandez clan and its associates joined Constanzo's cult.

While the cult had been no stranger to murder in the past, its new headquarters and the growing number of its members led to an increased sense of power and untouchability. Constanzo's previous belief that the bones of human sacrifice enabled higher powers now reached terrifying proportions. Beginning with the murders of other high-profile drug dealers, corrupt policemen and rival gang members, the cult soon began to carry out ritualistic murders at Matamoros. The victims were tortured and their body parts were boiled in the *nganga* before the concoction was drunk by the waiting members of the cult. Sometimes, necklaces were even crafted using pieces of the victim's spinal column.

Elio Hernandez was dubbed the "executioner priest", and Constanzo branded his chest and arms with sacred marks. At one stage, Hernandez was reported to have asked his followers to bring him a male victim for sacrifice, chopped off his head and then realized he had murdered one of his own nephews.

Unusually for the time, Constanzo was openly bisexual and took male and female lovers alike, many of whom were subsequently recruited into the cult. He was known as El Padrino (the Godfather). One of his new followers was a student called Sara Aldrete, who had grown up in a middle-class Mexican family and attended college in Texas, where she received excellent grades and was a member of the cheerleading squad. She was also, however, fascinated by the occult. Aldrete and Constanzo were soon dating, and she became known as La Madrina (the Godmother). She was his second in command, and it was Aldrete who oversaw operations at the cult when Constanzo was away, often on business trips shipping marijuana over the border from Mexico to the United States.

The mutilated remains of the cult's victims began to appear in and around Mexico City, and the Mexican press dubbed the cult "Los Narcosatánicos", although they were also known as the Matamoros Cult.

In 1989, Constanzo declared that the human sacrifices made so far were inadequate: for the ultimate spiritual power, the cult needed the brain of an American student. Mark Kilroy was a pre-medical student on spring break from his degree at the University of Texas at Austin. Kilroy was 19 years old at the time; he was born in Chicago, raised Catholic, an honours student at school and an active athlete, as well as a Boy Scout.

As the 1980s drew to a close, Kilroy had recently transferred to the new college with the aim of eventually sitting his Medical College Admission Test. He had travelled along with three friends to South Padre Island in Texas when his classes had finished on 10 March. The plan was to spend a few days at the beach and bar-hop over the border in the evenings: some 350,000 students did the same each year.

In the early hours of 14 March, Constanzo's henchmen abducted Kilroy from outside a bar in Matamoros and brought him to the Rancho Santa Elena. It is believed he was subsequently tortured and raped before being decapitated with a machete. His brain and spine were removed for the cult's hideous worship.

What Constanzo and his clan did not know was that Kilroy's uncle was an agent for the US Customs Service. Kilroy had failed to reconnect with his friends on the night of his abduction, and, as the days went by, concern for his well-being only increased. The police were bewildered but did not believe any serious harm could possibly have come to Kilroy, whose father issued a reward sum of $5,000. A US spokesman said that authorities had never had students reported missing on spring break before.

When one of the gang members drove past a police roadblock on 1 April, the authorities followed him all the way back to Rancho Santa Elena. When police searched the compound, they found some 65 lb of marijuana stashed across the house, and then they entered the shed containing the grisly *nganga*. Inside lay a dead black cat, a human brain and other unspecified and quickly decaying organs. According to reports at the time, Mexican police refused to continue exploring until a *curandero*, or healer, arrived to purify the entire site.

When interviewed, one of the property's caretakers recognized a photograph shown him by police; he started digging and soon exhumed Mark's dismembered corpse. To their astonishment, the day's hideous finds didn't stop there.

A total of 14 bodies were recovered across various burial sites at the ranch.

Just under a fortnight later, Elio Hernandez and three other cult members were in jail, confessing to the multiple murders. There was no sign, however, of Constanzo or his inner circle, including Sara Aldrete. On 6 May, Mexican police were called to a disturbance at an apartment in Mexico City. Little did they know that the persons involved were none other than fugitive members of Los Narcosatánicos. When Constanzo spotted the police car approaching, he started firing on them with a machine gun, reportedly crying that everything was lost. Over the next 45 minutes, gunfire cut across the buildings of the apartment block until Constanzo finally surrendered. He asked one of his followers to shoot him, an order that was promptly obeyed.

In 1994, Aldrete, who had escaped from the shoot-out alive but was subsequently arrested, was sentenced to over 60 years in prison, while Elio Hernandez was given 67. Other cult members were also incarcerated on a range of charges including drug smuggling, perverting the course of justice and murder.

POISON AND WATER

The summer of 1987 was a turbulent one for the people of South Korea. In June, pro-democracy protests were held across the country in a series of mass events that became known as the June Democratic Struggle. The military government was ultimately forced to reform its previous policies and introduce fair elections. This in turn led to the formation in October of that year of the Sixth Republic, which continues to rule South Korea to this day.

As August drew to a close, South Korean police were tightening the net around a known swindler, a woman called Park Soon-ja, who was said to have taken around ₩11.2 billion (£6.8 million) from over 200 people. Their investigations had brought them, on 29 August 1987, to a hidden factory in the mountains of Yongin, about 50 miles south of the country's capital Seoul.

It was here that, in the attic section of the building's cafeteria, a hideous discovery was made. Park was there, but she was dead, and so were 32 other people. The bodies were stacked on top of one another, their hands and feet bound and their mouths stuffed with cotton. Police staggered from the scene, retching and gasping for breath. However they had imagined they might find Park, the apparent fraudster, it was not like this.

On further examination, it was found the bodies had been dead for around two days. Police suspected quickly that the deaths were the result of a religious incident.

The events leading up to the summer of 1987 began with the formation of the Evangelical Baptist Church of Korea (EBC). It was established in 1962 by Yoo Byung-eun, and across South Korea the Church is more commonly known as Guwonpa (Salvation Sect). It remains active to this day, though exact membership numbers are hazy. It was later proclaimed a cult in 1992 by the General Assembly, who declared it was heretical, but this was later revoked to suggest the EBC's beliefs as being consistent with Christianity.

While Buddhism was once dominant in South Korea, the past decades have seen a marked interest and eventual overtaking of the traditional religion, and the Christian faith is now more popular. Interestingly, the specific beliefs of Korean Christians place a large emphasis on evangelizing and spreading the word through overseas missions, and in fact the only country that has a higher rate of such activities is the United States. There is also a long-standing tradition of congregants paying the Church sometimes as much as 10 per cent of their salaries. For some more cunning "entrepreneurs", there was a clear and socially sanctioned method of money-making here.

Little is known of Park's life before the events of this grim story but she is thought to have defected from the Salvation Sect at some point in the 1970s or early 1980s. Park founded the Five Oceans, a craftwork manufacturer that became well known across South Korea for hiring impoverished artisans.

Park developed a reputation for philanthropy and good deeds, an image strengthened by her neat haircut, wide smile and pressed clothes, not to mention the fact that her husband,

Lee Kee-jung, was a senior provincial government official. She was a socialite, a trusted member of South Korea's metropolitan elite, and her employees spoke highly of her. She also ran a charity for orphans and elderly homeless people within the city of Daejeon.

If there were clues as to Park's true nature and intentions, they were well hidden. One answer may lie in the name of Five Oceans, or Odaeyang Trading. It would emerge later that Park had long harboured visions of ruling the world through a new belief system splintered from the original Evangelical Baptist Church.

The handicraft manufacturing business was a mere front for the group's real work. While claiming to be Christian, the group preached that the world was due to end imminently and only adherence to the cult's teachings, plus obedience to Park, would guarantee salvation when the end arrived. Park had explained to her followers that God had spoken to her, telling her to gather a flock of devotees to prepare for the world's end. Having been diagnosed with, treated for and then cured of cancer, she also claimed that God had rid her of the disease.

Park purchased a factory in the isolated mountains of Yongin and, to the outside world, made a decent living from the tourist-souvenir manufacturing undertaken there. Her followers called her "Benevolent Mother". As time went on, she began to extract money from them, demanding what she described as loans necessitated by the costs of spreading God's word and maintaining her charitable donations. The amount of money handed over increased exponentially, and over 200 people, usually employees of the company or their family members, were the main sources of "income".

On 16 August 1987, police received notification that two members of the public who had recently donated money to the Odaeyang cult had been beaten by Park's followers when they'd demanded it back. Over time, more and more employees of the company were arrested on suspicion of similar beatings. Those who had once been aided by Park's charity work, like the elderly, homeless and children, were often targeted either for cash or unpaid labour in the Yongin factory.

As police continued to explore enquiries against Park, they decided to examine her business premises, leading to 29 August. Heavily armed officers surrounded the factory as the first agents entered the property. As they heard and saw nothing, they moved from room to room, weapons held aloft. All was silent.

When they came pouring out of the factory, their faces pale, the officers described unimaginable horror. There were bodies stacked in two piles: 14 in one, 19 in the other. Strangely, many of the dead were wearing only underwear or pyjamas. What had happened here?

Television networks descended on the scene, and soon South Korea watched in rapt attention as the victims of the atrocity were removed from the attic. The first reports described bruising on the necks of the dead, while others claimed they had been poisoned; their hands and feet had also been bound. Bizarrely, despite the death toll, there was little to no evidence of violence or resistance. Rubber gloves and glass medicine bottles were found beside the piles of bodies.

Forensic experts arrived to analyse the attic and discovered evidence of human habitation: there were several plastic boxes filled with human waste, cans of food, noodles, knives, forks, spoons, hymn books, a Bible, handbags and clothing. Notes were also found close to the bodies. "The president or someone else went for poison and water," one read.

DESTRUCTIVE CULTS

As appalling as the story was, it was far from unique in the region. Religious sects flourished during the twentieth century in Korea, and often focused on a leader whose charisma and charm went hand in hand alongside their own business opportunities and personal wealth. Many new and often secretive organizations sprang up during that century's period of turbulence and instability, with profit the major motivator behind a veil of pious spiritualism. The followers of these new religions were largely female, often lonely widows with a pension left over from their deceased husbands. Once the followers had been indoctrinated by the cult leader, they would hand over their possessions and undertake work for free.

Between the years 1910 and 1945, the country was occupied as a Japanese colony. Just five years later the Korean War erupted, with decades of military dictatorship following the mass unrest and bloodshed that time brought about. As with other examples, the ideologies of new religious movements gave a clear and unequivocal method of living with a deified leader, who offered seeming solidity and certainty. However bad the outside world might seem, these new belief systems promised salvation. Between the 1960s and 1990s, some 400 religious groups were born, with the majority appearing in the 1980s as the nation's military dictatorship began to end.

In 1982, for example, Kim Gi-sun founded a cult in which she claimed she was a sinless *aga* (baby); she attracted many hundreds of followers and ran a farm and a large record store in Seoul. Both were managed and run by "volunteers" who were unpaid and who had given their own assets, however meagre, to Kim. It would later emerge that those who defected or who attempted to "slander" the leader were often murdered and their bodies buried.

Even the Salvation Sect from which Odaeyang sprang was not without blemish, with its founder Yoo Byung-eun setting up a trading firm called Semo Group in 1979; this enabled him to steadily grow his personal wealth to an astonishing £143 million.

So what happened at the Odaeyang factory? Autopsies were conducted on the bodies and it was revealed that Park, her children and the majority of her followers had swallowed an unknown drug prior to death or inhaled it through the cotton found in their mouths. This likely incapacitated the group, who were then strangled to death. The South Korean public were soon aghast at this apparent murder-suicide, with one or more members tasked with dosing the devotees before strangling them and then taking their own lives. One man, the factory manager, was found hanged, apparently by his own hand.

The idea that some of the factory's employees had been hiding with Park was confirmed by a maid who worked at the factory, who explained to police that the leader and her devotees had been in hiding since the Wednesday prior. A fight had broken out, it seemed, between the company's employees and a creditor who had come to ask for repayment of a debt. The maid said she had brought a meal to the leader once a day but hadn't seen her since Friday. The youngest of the victims was just 17 years old.

The entire belief system behind Odaeyang had been an elaborate ruse for Park's business model. The poor and needy had been manipulated into handing over all they owned, often with high interest rates attached that steadily put Park into unmanageable debt. Creditors were promised repayment that never materialized. Finally realizing that the police were on the case, she took matters into her own, bloody hands.

NIGHT AND DAY

The Knights Templar was a twelfth-century order endorsed by the Pope and renowned for its military prowess and wealth. They are credited with developing early banking systems and building fortifications across Europe and the Holy Land, and were instrumental to the pioneering missions of the Crusades. In 1307, as rumours spread about the initiation systems inherent to the order's membership, King Philip IV of France pressured Pope Clement V to have French members of the Templars arrested, tortured and burned at the stake.

In 1805, a Parisian doctor called Bernard-Raymond Fabré-Palaprat claimed to be the Templars' head, declaring that he was the successor in a long line of grand masters. Throughout the years of the knights' persecution, he said, his forefathers had kept the medieval order alive and hidden it from the public; now, he had arrived to bring about a resurgence of that order. This new phase of the group split into many different sections and some of the latest iterations held strong beliefs about the imminent end of the world.

One such member was Luc Jouret. He was born in 1947 in what was then the Belgian Congo, but returned as a child to his parents' native Belgium, where he gained a medical degree from the Vrije Universiteit Brussel (VUB) in 1974. He was a staunch communist during his adolescence and student days, and subsequently joined the Belgian army as a paratrooper. After this, he qualified as a homeopathic specialist and began to practise in France. He made a point of travelling across the world, from China to Peru and India, to examine and study different forms of medicine, including alternative healing customs, the paranormal and spiritualism.

In 1984, Jouret founded the Ordre du Temple solaire (Order of the Solar Temple) along with Joseph Di Mambro, a French jeweller and horologist. As a young man, Di Mambro had joined the Ancient and Mystical Order of the Rosae Crucis and had since set up several of his own organizations, one of which was the Golden Way Foundation. This was where the pair had met, with Jouret having lectured at the Geneva-based foundation.

The new group was an offshoot of the Renewed Order of the Temple, which claimed its descent from the Templars. The pair managed the new group together, with Di Mambro taking a less prominent, public-facing role and allowing Jouret to serve as its primary recruiter. Jouret began to move between different countries in Europe, as well as Tenerife, Martinique and Canada, to preach his messages.

The Solar Temple believed firmly in the notion that the world was headed for destruction – exactly how was unclear – at some point in the 1990s. In many ways, therefore, this was a doomsday cult such as those we will detail in the next chapter: devotees believed that in order to survive the apocalypse they needed to attain the highest plane of spirituality and human understanding. The group's members believed that the world's population needed to prepare for the transition of the Second Coming of Christ as a solar god-king, and that religious faiths such as Christianity and Islam needed to unite to achieve the transition.

That wasn't all – the Temple was also known to incorporate elements of belief in UFOs and tailored Freemason rituals. Its purported links to the grand masters of the Templars lent it a legitimacy steeped in ancient ritual; it was Di Mambro who assigned certain followers the task of bringing the so-called New Age to the rest of the world, to spread the message of the coming apocalypse. The group's members believed that they alone would produce the next generation of "cosmic children". Di Mambro would further these beliefs by claiming members had lived previous lives, often as famous people.

As time went on, Solar Temple facilities or "lodges" were established in the Quebec towns of Morin-Heights and Sainte-Anne-de-la-Pérade. They were also known to have followings in Australia, Switzerland and the French colony of Martinique. These were run by regional commanders, as well as "Elders", and members were given different grades, known as the Brothers of Parvis, the Knights of the Alliance, and the Brothers of the Ancient Times.

The group's headquarters was moved to Zürich, where it was overseen by a council of 33 members known as the Elder Brothers of the Rosy Cross. For the next stage of the group's plan, its leaders devised a programme of occult practices and rituals that would in turn allow the Great White Brotherhood – beings of great power who spread spiritual knowledge through some chosen men and women – to bring about the New Age.

The group had its own altars and costumes. Ceremonies of initiation included the payment of joining fees, while other members wore robes and covers reminiscent of the Templars' clothing. During these ceremonies, depending on where they were held, a sword was presented to members, which Di Mambro claimed was a Templar relic that had been given to him in a previous life 1,000 years before.

Throughout the 1980s, Jouret's new sect flourished. At its height, it boasted 442 members, many of whom had originally been followers of other New Age religions. In 1982, Di Mambro's newborn daughter Emmanuelle was assigned as a messiah for the New Age. Now the group had not only followers, international lodges and money, but a successor.

It wasn't until the 1990s that several unfortunate events coincided to bring about dissidence within the group. Di Mambro became unwell, members began to trickle away and police across the different countries where the Solar Temple operated started investigations into the cult's activities. In addition, several previous members demanded that the money they'd paid the group be reimbursed. When Jouret was arrested trying to buy handguns with silencers in Quebec, the media took the story and ran with it. Overnight, the former medical student and homeopathic expert's reputation was tarnished. In Australia, in 1993, Jouret and Di Mambro, among others, lamented the fact that their efforts were proving ever more futile. They put in place a series of documents to be posted in October of the following year, which would detail their justification for what came next.

By 1994, the situation had worsened further. Members continued to leave, and both Jouret and Di Mambro decided that, since the world refused to listen, they would escape it and enact a perfect revenge on the detractors and deserters. Around the same time, a follower called Nicky Dutoit became pregnant, something that was explicitly against the cult's rules by this point. She and her husband, Tony, left the cult, distressed by the reaction this news elicited from the Elders. Their son, Christopher Emmanuel, was born. Fearing for the successor status of his own daughter, Emmanuelle, Di Mambro immediately claimed the child as "the Antichrist" – in other words, Satan incarnate.

When the baby was three months old, assassins entered the Dutoit family home by night. It is believed that Di Mambro ordered the murder of the infant, which was carried out using a wooden stake. The boy's parents were also killed before the two Solar Temple hitmen took their own lives.

On 3 October 1994, the Solar Temple's two founders joined several other members of the cult in an extravagant banquet in Switzerland. They ate at a local restaurant and regarded the occasion as a "last supper", such as that taken by Jesus and his disciples the night before his crucifixion.

At some point soon afterwards, a series of mass suicides and murders took place at three ski chalets in the villages of Cheiry and Salvan in western Switzerland. Police later found letters written by the Solar Temple's followers, which stated their belief that they were leaving the "hypocrisies and oppression of this world". Among the dead were a mayor, a journalist and a civil servant. Quebec police began to uncover enormous donations, some of over C$1 million (£600,000), which wealthier members had given over to the order.

At Morin-Heights, where one of the lodges was based, 15 of the members' innermost circle took their own lives using poison, while 30 were either shot or smothered to death. At Cheiry, 18 dead members were discovered with their bodies arranged in a circle, dressed in the cult's ceremonial robes and with plastic bags tied over their heads: this was believed to be a symbolic gesture referencing the group's belief in an environmental catastrophe that would soon befall the earth. At one of the sites, bodies were discovered in an underground chapel covered with mirrors.

After the suicides took place, some of the buildings were set on fire using remote-controlled devices. It would later be ruled that of the 52 dead members, just 15 had actively taken their own lives: most had been drugged and then shot. Di Mambro and Jouret were among the dead.

If appalled authorities believed this to be the grisly conclusion to the cult's activities, they were wrong. In 1995, a further 16 members took their own lives near Grenoble in France: two were found to have shot the remaining 14 before turning their weapons on themselves or, gruesomely, setting themselves on fire. Edith Bonlieu, who had competed in the Alpine skiing division of the 1956 Winter Olympics in Italy, was among the dead. In March 1997, on the spring equinox, a further five members took their own lives when their house was set on fire; police discovered their charred bodies, and later recovered a group of children and teenagers in a garden shed, all of whom had been drugged but had survived.

After these shocking resurgences in violent mass murder and suicide, the Solar Temple was gradually disbanded in the years that followed. The notoriety of the case led to a new and fundamental mistrust in both France and Belgium where New Age sects were concerned. When the Swiss government launched a review into the deaths, it found that they were directly linked to the Solar Temple's religious ideologies.

FAMILY TIES

In 1993, both Interpol and the FBI were chasing the same man. In fact, they'd been chasing him for two decades, on child abuse and kidnapping charges. He had since proved frustratingly elusive, protected by a shield of followers determined to ensure his liberty. Even when capture seemed imminent, ex-followers of the fugitive man were legally obstructed from testifying in court, proof was hard to come by and current followers denied any allegation of wrongdoing on the part of their leader.

Elsewhere, in the same year, a young man called River Phoenix, an American actor and musician, was found convulsing on a Los Angeles sidewalk. He was rushed to hospital but attempts to resuscitate him were unsuccessful and he was formally pronounced dead in the early hours of Halloween, aged just 23. His death was caused by a drug overdose of both cocaine and heroin.

River Phoenix was born in 1970 and was the eldest of five children. His younger sisters included Rain, Liberty and Summer Phoenix; Joaquin, his brother, has since been named by the *New York Times* as one of the greatest actors of the twenty-first century. The children had an unconventional start to life, however. When River was three years old, his parents joined a religious organization that was known, at the time, as the Children of God; they were stationed in Caracas, in Venezuela, and were given work as missionaries and fruit pickers.

They would eventually leave in 1977, but the damage had at that point been done. In a magazine interview published in late 1991, River Phoenix claimed that he had lost his virginity as a small child, at the age of four, to other children who were also members of the Children of God.

A year after Phoenix's death, the man so heavily sought after by various police forces around the world died in Portugal. His name was David Berg.

Berg was born in 1919 and grew up to become a pastor with the Alliance World Fellowship, or Christian and Missionary Alliance. This Protestant group is evangelical in its beliefs, and its key aim is Christian perfection and union with God, or "perfect love". In 1968, Berg had gathered a small following as a preacher at a coffee shop in Orange County, California. The majority of this new group, then called Teens for Christ, were self-described hippies dedicated to the free love movement that had sprung up over several Western countries within the space of a decade.

Berg soon explained that the state would duly be decimated by an earthquake and left the area with his devotees. At this point, the group's name was changed to the Children of God, and Berg claimed he alone was the prophet to spread the word of the Lord and announce the imminent apocalypse or End Times. Through street preaching and the distribution of pamphlets, his following grew steadily and soon small communes were being established beyond the state of California.

Berg styled himself Moses David, and by the early 1970s, just four years after the cult's foundation, the Children of

God had 130 communities across 70 countries, with around 10,000 full-time members. These members often dressed in nothing more than sackcloths and demonstrated in the streets to draw attention to the country's perceived rejection of God and Christian principles. The necessity of leaving the United States was not only due to the nation's apparent godlessness, but also for the sect to find new members around the world. In the meantime, a series of letters – some 30,000 across the course of Berg's rule – were mailed out describing the sect's aims, missions and the importance of gathering new followers. These were known as "Mo Letters" and, later, "The New Good News". Berg was stationed in Portugal, far away from the prying eyes of the US government.

While some members lived on purpose-built communes, usually on isolated farms, others lived in their own homes, mixing only with other members who also lived locally. If a local or national newspaper published reports about the group, they would either use the publicity to garner new members or simply move away if the press was too negative. On some farmsteads, families didn't have access to toilets, showers or electricity. They had no possessions, grew their own crops and were surrounded by farm animals; children were usually bathed in barrels. Their days were spent tending to the land, praying and reading, or going out to preach in villages, towns and cities nearby.

While the sect might have been considered strange or New Age in its belief systems up until now, 1976 marked a turning point. Berg now described the need for what he termed "flirty fishing", which persuaded female members of the Children of God to demonstrate their devotion to the Lord through sex with people they were trying to recruit. This precipitated the addition of new converts, often lonely men who were targeted in the belief they would be more likely to join the sect as a result. Sex was seen as a service to the Lord, and pamphlets featured images of topless or fully naked women; the Holy Spirit was depicted as a goddess in a heart-shaped bikini.

Using the pre-existing drive for self-expression and unconventionality sweeping the rest of the country at the time, Berg advocated for members to liberate themselves from "taboos". Two years after the introduction of flirty fishing tactics, the sect was rebranded once more, this time as "The Family".

In 1980, one of the Mo Letters, number 999 from May, was sent out with the headline "The Devil Hates Sex! But God Loves It!". Statistics later compiled by a researcher examining The Family's practices estimated that members had sex with almost 224,000 different people.

Scotland had Family sites across the country, including in Renfrewshire, Lanarkshire, Ayrshire and Edinburgh. One ex-member described the abuse she suffered at the hands of other followers, abuse dating back to when she was four. "It became hell on earth for anyone born into it," said Verity Carter, who was born into the communal lifestyle of The Family. "It happened a step at a time and many of the adults did not see how extreme it had got until it was too late. A lot of parents did leave and take their kids out."

Carter's father left The Family before she turned ten, but she and her siblings stayed behind with their mother. She described a total lack of contact with the outside world, no music or television and no knowledge of how things like school, the government, shopping centres, museums, holidays or the job market worked. She and other children her age were taught to guard the secrets of The Family closely from so-called "systemites"; they didn't receive any formal schooling but were taught survival skills instead. Children's colouring books showed diagrams of genitals and illustrations of copulating couples.

Meanwhile, the cult became the target of paedophiles, who observed an opportunity to commit their crimes within the socially accepted confines of a faith movement. It was reported that the herpes virus spread across the cult's membership. Berg changed tactic once more and proclaimed that the children of members were to experience a wholesome atmosphere; rules relating to the protection of children were introduced, and flirty fishing tactics were forbidden.

Aiming to garner a sense of legitimacy, Berg ejected over 300 members of the sect at this point, citing "serious misconduct and abuse of their position". Some of these exiled followers had objected to the flirty fishing tactic that had been widely used across different missionary expeditions around the world. It was at this stage in the group's evolution that serious concerns were raised about the "free love" philosophy espoused by Berg and his inner circle.

Reports of child abuse and the rape of minors became the focal point of ire directed at Berg and The Family, with around an eighth of the total membership leaving in protest. The Parents' Committee to Free Our Children from the Children of God was established as an "anti-cult" organization, dedicated to preventing child abuse within sects such as Berg's.

In March 1989, a statement was issued reminding members that sexual contact between adults and children was "strictly forbidden". Anyone found to have engaged in such practices, The Family claimed, would be excommunicated. The group publicly renounced abortion, homosexuality, drugs and drink in an effort to present itself in a better, more Christian-centric light.

Alarmed by reports emerging from ex-members, the police began a series of raids at homes of Family members, but little evidence of abuse was discovered. A *Washington Post* journalist called Gustav Niebuhr was invited to visit the commune in La Habra, California, perhaps in an effort to restore a semblance of credibility and positivity where the cult was concerned. Niebuhr described the members he encountered as "a clean-cut bunch, friendly and courteous".

Upon Berg's death in October 1994, his wife Maria took up leadership of The Family and set out a new "Love Charter" describing the group's constitution, rights and rules. The focus shifted away from free love, sex or "breaking taboos", and some members returned. To this day, some 10,000 followers exist in around 90 countries.

DOOMSDAY CULTS

The concept of the End Times has existed since the dawn of humanity. Early civilizations had no inkling of modern scientific methods of investigation: no seasonal charts, maps of the universe, no notion of the cosmos beyond what they could see. The fear, therefore, that all life – human, animal and plant – could be instantaneously wiped out was both real and understandable. As time passed, academic research into the big bang theory and the world's creation often bumped up against long-held religious beliefs. The idea that all life is nothing more than a collection of cells – accidentally grouped together and which evolved over millions of years – seemed at odds with the notion of a divine, omnipotent creator with a plan and a design.

As such, many new organizations over the centuries have promised enlightenment through access to information about the world's end. For the leaders of these groups, who often present themselves as the intermediary between God and mankind, strict observance of certain rules and beliefs must be wholeheartedly adopted as Armageddon approaches. Many natural disasters, from earthquakes to the eruption of volcanoes, floods, plagues and pandemics, are seen as clear evidence by such cults of our impending doom. Particularly throughout the twentieth century, with seismic events such as both World Wars, the Holocaust, the atomic bombs at Hiroshima and Nagasaki, the wars in Korea and Vietnam, the Cold War, the 1969 moon landings, the assassination of John F. Kennedy and the fall of the Berlin Wall, many around the world felt that chaos and destruction of the planet was not only likely, but certain.

Doomsday cults rely on a deep and primal fear within us all. In March 2023, reports emerged from the deep forests of Shakahola, in Kenya, where 22 bodies were discovered, adding to an ever-growing number that now stands at 201. The Good News International Church is currently under investigation for its calls for members to starve themselves to death. This, it is claimed, enables followers to reach heaven before the End Times. It has been a stark and dreadful reminder of such groups' power and the desperate devotion experienced by followers.

WHAT'S IN THE BOX?

The market town of Bedford lies about 50 miles north of London. It is home to a motte, or mound of earth, on which sat an impressive ancient castle built around 1100 by Henry I, and a fortress commissioned by the Anglo-Saxon king Edward the Elder; both sites look out over the River Ouse. The town is therefore of historical interest dating back almost a millennium. In the past century, however, it has attracted a new focus of touristic intrigue. Somewhere in Bedford, hidden safely away in an undisclosed location, a large wooden trunk is sitting locked, its latches securely fastened and ropes criss-crossing its long frame.

This mysterious box was believed to have contained prophecies and has never been opened since it was sealed at some point in the 1830s. During the 1920s and 1930s, the Panacea Society (more on them shortly) worked hard to persuade Anglican bishops around the UK to open the box. Some 100,000 signatures were even gathered for petitions to be presented to the clergy following a highly successful media campaign across regional and national newspapers.

Although it was officially founded in 1919, the Panacea Society was inspired by the teachings of a woman called Joanna Southcott, who was born in 1750. Southcott wrote and dictated many prophecies through the course of her life, and claimed to be the Virgin Mary, or "Woman of the Apocalypse". She came to London and sold "seals of the Lord" for cash, promising eternal life as a result. At the age of 64, she announced that she was pregnant with a new messiah, and her now dedicated followers, around 100,000 Londoners, were persuaded of this due to the fact Southcott did indeed look pregnant. The baby never appeared, however.

Southcott died in 1814 and left the box behind with a single, express decree. It could only be opened, by all 24 Anglican bishops, during a time of national crisis. And so it was that Mabel Barltrop, the widow of a curate (a priest's assistant) from Bedford, came to state in 1919 that she was the "Daughter of God" whose role had once been filled by Southcott.

Mabel Andrews was born in Peckham, south-east London, and married Arthur Henry Barltrop in 1889. Arthur had completed his ministerial training the year before and the couple went on to have four children. The family moved to Bedford after the onset of Arthur's illness – the details of which are unclear – in 1902; he died four years later, and Mabel spent a brief spell being treated for what was then known as melancholia, a type of depression.

Life was hard and full of worry for the now widowed Mabel, and it was at around this time that she read a leaflet written by one of Southcott's followers, Alice Seymour, who would organize the publication of Southcott's works – barring the hidden prophecies in the box – but it was Mabel who began, with other local women, to call on bishops and oversee the opening of the box.

The second decade of the 1900s was, indeed, a time of crisis. For four long years World War One brought untold tragedy to countless families in the UK, Germany and other nations across the world. Fighting was still ongoing, with armistice some eight months away when the first case of the H1N1 influenza virus was documented in Kansas. By April, cases were recorded in Europe, and by 1920 a third of the world's population had been infected with the virus.

The disease was exponentially deadly with high mortality rates among the young, and it ravaged the globe in four successive waves that killed somewhere between 17 million and 50 million people. Suddenly, the already beleaguered medical services dealing with the war-wounded were attempting to curb the spread of the highly infectious variant, and makeshift hospitals were soon overcrowded incubators of the disease. Many hundreds of nurses became victims of the virus.

Millenarism comes from the Latin word *millenarius* (containing a thousand), and its belief structure focuses on the idea of society's transformation through a crisis or apocalyptic event. After the event itself, believers state that a new paradise will emerge. The Panacea Society was founded on this principle and believed that it held the answers to the impending state of Armageddon the world was about to enter.

Mabel Barltrop was christened "Octavia" by her initial followers, and as time went on word spread. The first headquarters was at 12 Albany Road, close to the ancient motte of Bedford Castle. Octavia and the 12 apostles called themselves the Community of the Holy Ghost. Nearby stood another house, also on Albany Road, which was termed "The Ark" and set aside as a messianic residence to be used after the Second Coming.

The traditional Christian Trinity was reconstructed from a triangle to a square, allowing Octavia her place as the Daughter of God. For her devoted followers, it was Eve who had first brought sin into the world, and therefore only a woman could banish it forever and usher in a new age. In 1923, Octavia announced that Arthur, her husband, had in fact been Jesus incarnate, and so the group was waiting for the third coming of the Messiah.

New members began to leave their homes, sometimes travelling for hours on end to arrive in Bedford to take up residence in a group of unassuming red-brick Victorian town houses. The houses looked on to a small chapel and a garden that members believed to be the original location of the Garden of Eden. It appears to have been self-sufficient, with allotments for growing food.

In the 1920s and 1930s, there were around 70 members of the Panacea Society, all of them women and most of them of middle-class background. The majority were over the age of 40 and had been raised at the end of the Victorian age, when conservative values were held in the highest of regards. Since many were unmarried, the Society appeared to offer a sense of purpose and power to a demographic largely unrepresented in Britain at the time; women couldn't vote or enter the clergy themselves, but in this way they could found their own religious order that had been legitimized by an older single woman.

In 1927, a box that appeared similar to the one cherished by the Society was opened in uncertain circumstances, but it was found to contain nothing but a lottery ticket and a broken pistol. The Society's campus continued to grow, however, and its members constructed high walls around their houses to ensure their protection from an increasingly frightening and morally bankrupt world.

Besides campaigning for the unsealing of the box, the Panacea Society offered healthcare solutions to subscribers, who could write to the Bedford headquarters. In turn, they would receive a square of linen that had been blessed by Octavia, in addition to a promise that this would cure disease including cancer and sometimes even provide eternal life.

It is estimated that some 120,000 requests of this kind were made to the Society from people all over the world. Those who had requested help were told to place the linen in a jug of water and pray before drinking the solution four times a day; once diluted this would become "Water B", for use in washing the body. There was no cost associated with the postage of the blessed linen, but participants were asked to confirm whether the treatment had been successful. For this reason, it is unclear exactly where the Society's wealth stemmed from. It was, perhaps, funded in part by the personal incomes or inheritance of its members, as the society owned several different properties. Decades later in 2001, it began to sell some of these houses so that it could keep its charity status; its assets were valued at around £14 million.

In 1934, Octavia died from diabetes in Bedford. For three days, the Panacea Society kept her body warm in the belief that she was not truly dead or, if she was, that she would come back to life. On the third day, however, they were forced to admit defeat and Octavia was buried; the message on her gravestone simply read "I am the Resurrection and the Life".

Despite the death of their leader, as the years went by the Society continued to invite bishops to stay at its headquarters. They provided accommodation and continued to furnish the second house on Albany Lane for Christ's third coming. On 4 September 1939, the day after Britain declared war on Germany, the group placed an announcement in the *Daily Telegraph*. "Notice to Sealed Members and Water

Takers," it read, "should a state of emergency arise whereby communication with Head Quarters is interrupted or becomes difficult, continue to fill your bottle with Water as required and repeat the Blessing. Sprinkle your Houses."

Despite the increased seriousness of the geopolitical situation, newspapers and magazines began to poke fun at the society and its beliefs, particularly when it started commissioning billboards encouraging the country's bishops to travel to Bedford and open the box. This, they felt, would save the country and avert the coming End Days.

Although membership dwindled in the 1940s, the group appeared to still be active 30 years later. More billboards appeared at this time: "War, disease, crime and banditry, distress of nations and perplexity," they stated, "will increase until the Bishops open Joanna Southcott's box."

The Society's last member was Ruth Klein, who died in 2012 at the age of 80. From that point, the Panacea was no more. Instead, the charity announced it would open a museum dedicated to the society's history, which is still operational to this day. It also funds research into other prophetic or millenarian movements. The original houses form the location of the Panacea Museum, which tells the story of the cult and its belief systems. The museum shows the houses used by the society with very little change, from the smart drawing rooms to the replica box on display. It contains, among much else, a golden cradle and embroidered baby clothes for the messiah Southcott declared she was due to bear.

ANT-EATERS

The Seventh-day Adventist Church developed from the mid-nineteenth century in the United States, being recognized in 1863. It shares much with more mainstream Christian doctrine. Its members believe in the sanctity of the Holy Trinity and follow the lessons of the Bible, and the Church has over 21 million baptized members.

Where it differs from other branches of Protestantism is its focus on the Second Coming of Christ and belief in the Last Judgement: the moment that God will smite heathens and the damned, obliterating them completely instead of condemning them to hell. Once the Last Judgement takes place, says the Church, we will see the Great Tribulation, a period of chaos and turmoil that will herald Christ's advent on Earth. With such a wide and international congregation, the Seventh-day Adventist Church is managed at a local level by individual regions and divisions within specific countries. However, as is so often the case with such large followings, the potential for new and sometimes disturbing sects operating within the original framework of the religion is high.

Roch Thériault was born in 1947 in Saguenay, a Quebec city in eastern Canada. Like many families in the area, the

Thériaults were French Canadian. As a boy, Thériault was regarded as highly capable academically but, for unknown reasons, he left school at the age of 12 and began to educate himself. This took the form of reading, understanding and following the key principles of the Bible's Old Testament. He soon converted from his native Catholicism to the Seventh-day Adventist Church and became convinced that the world was to end imminently.

In the earliest days of his new belief system, Thériault appears to have primarily abided by the Adventist belief in healthy living, consuming only whole foods and avoiding such teenage temptations as alcohol or tobacco. He was later described as charming, persuasive and likeable. In spite of the radical nature of his departure from traditional education, his parents considered that the decision – and the motivations behind it – were at least wholesome, if slightly odd.

By the mid-1970s, however, Thériault decided to pursue a new, different path of religious self-expression. He was a skilled orator and had been conducting motivational speeches, which resulted in the development of a small group of followers. There were just 12 adults in total and a handful of children. As time went on, he convinced them to resign from their jobs and sell their belongings for cash. They must join him, he said, in a dedicated group that would branch off from the Seventh-day Adventists; many of the new group were former members. His group, called the Ant Hill Kids, was formed in 1977 in Sainte-Marie, Quebec; he was thus expelled from the Church.

Thériault claimed that he was the prophet Moses reincarnated and could perform miracles. He also stated that God had warned him that the world would end in February 1979, and only those who followed him could hope to survive.

At his commune, members were informed they would live among one another in harmony, free from sin and with total equality. However, to join they were required to cut ties with their families and with any previous religious affiliation. In 1978, the Ant Hill Kids relocated to the Gaspé Peninsula, a remote region of some 12,000 square miles – fittingly, its name derives from the Mi'kmaq word for "end". There, the tiny village of Saint-Jogues became the group's "Eternal Mountain", and it was here Thériault decided to base his followers in preparation for the apocalypse

It was at this time, while his followers set about constructing their commune, that Thériault christened his movement the Ant Hill Kids. He compared members to ants busily carrying materials and supplies to their anthill. Instead of the promised equality the group had been relying on, women were instructed to be subservient to the male members of the group and polygamy was encouraged. Thériault insisted on being called "Father" or "Papy", and chose new names for the individuals working to construct the Eternal Mountain settlement. Initially, the group appears to have made its money through baking, selling the goods to local villages and towns.

From the inception of the cult, Thériault insisted on his divine right to multiple wives and "concubines", and fathered 26 children in total, by every one of his female members. The women – Solange, Gabrielle, Chantal, Marise, Josée, Francine, Nicole and Gisèle – were forced to worship Thériault and follow his every order. The Ant Hill Kids soon grew in number and Thériault maintained absolute control over all members, with severe punishments for any perceived disobedience or wrongdoing. Followers believed, wholeheartedly, that Thériault alone was a righteous, benevolent deity sent to protect them from Armageddon, and that they themselves were full of sin.

While he had eschewed alcohol growing up, Thériault now had a drinking problem and his measures of group control were becoming increasingly strange. Soon, members were dressed in identical tunics and were banned from even speaking to one another without their leader being present. Paranoia gripped the commune's members and was exacerbated by the punishments he meted out.

Followers were whipped and beaten with belts and hammers; sometimes they were even nailed to trees and suspended from ceilings. Thériault would insist on plucking their body hair individually, removing their fingernails or teeth to maximize their pain, and was known even to defecate on anyone who broke the rules. He would force his followers to break their own legs with sledgehammers, shoot one another and eat vermin.

February 1979 came and went, but there was no indication the apocalypse was about to occur. Thériault waved this problem away and claimed that earthly and divine time were not parallel – there had simply been a mistake when God gave the month and year of doomsday. Scepticism increased among the community, but by this point Thériault's total control was well established and there were some 40 members of the Ant Hill Kids, many of them children. Parents were naturally wary of angering their cult leader and risking harm to either themselves or their children.

In 1984, the group moved to a new settlement near Burnt River in Central Ontario. The terrible abuse continued, and nobody was spared. Gabrielle Lavallée, one of the leaders' "wives", realized her newborn would be subjected to the same sexual abuse experienced by other children at the commune;

she left her baby outside to die in the cold rather than risk the child with Thériault. Realizing, perhaps, that there was increasing dissidence towards his rule, the leader increased his punishments and "purifications". This took the form of conducting surgery on the group, performing circumcisions and injecting ethanol into their stomachs. Fear was the reigning factor and any members who voiced their desire to leave were tortured to within an inch of their lives.

Rumours began to circulate about the terrible practices being inflicted on the Ant Hill Kids. In 1987, social workers arrived at the new compound and removed 17 children into their care. Shockingly, Thériault was neither questioned nor arrested: the cult's status as a Church protected it from the "interference" of authorities and thus enabled its abuses to continue.

Lavallée, the mother who had left her baby outside, continued to receive especially harsh punishments, including having a welding torch applied to her genitals. Eight of her teeth had also been removed and, when she tried to escape, Thériault mutilated her by cutting off her breast and hitting her with an axe. He also removed one of her fingers and amputated her arm. Incredibly, despite these horrific injuries, Lavallée managed to escape successfully in 1989, and she called the police.

Finally, the police were able to act. Thériault was arrested, charged with assault and sentenced to 12 years in prison. Once their leader had been removed, the Ant Hill Kids quickly disbanded and Lavallée was instrumental in wider investigations into the dreadful happenings at both compounds. In 1993, Thériault was convicted of the murder of Solange Boilard, another of his wives, whom he had murdered in 1989. Boilard had complained of stomach pains and, after a gruesome botched amateur surgery performed without anaesthetic, she died the following day. Thériault attempted to resurrect the woman he himself had killed by sawing off the top of her skull and masturbating into it. When this didn't work, Boilard was buried close to the compound.

For this crime, Thériault pled guilty and was sentenced to life imprisonment. Incredibly, three of his former wives maintained contact with him during this time and he fatherered more children with two of them as a result of permitted conjugal visits. In 2009, he attempted to sell some of his artwork to a site calling itself a "true crime auction house", but was thwarted by the Correctional Service of Canada. Two years later, he was murdered by his cellmate, who stabbed him in the neck before informing guards: "That piece of shit is down on the range. Here's the knife, I've sliced him up." The terrible rule of Roch Thériault was finally at an end.

MIDNIGHT WENT

It was 29 October 1992. A normal day for most, and an unthinkable tragedy for a small minority. This was never supposed to happen. The earth was still turning. People headed into work for the day, dogs barked, buses stopped to pick up passengers and drop them off. It was incomprehensible for the hundreds of thousands of followers who had been convinced the day before was to be their last on Earth.

Just before midnight that day, police waited with bated breath outside the Dami Mission church in the South Korean capital of Seoul. They had been sent, in force, to manage the scenes expected to take place; there were 1,500 riot officers and 200 detectives present, dressed in plain clothes. Reporters had flocked from around the country to witness events play out. They'd been there since 7 p.m., reporting on the gatherings taking place across Dami Mission churches around the country. Furniture had even been set on fire by followers outside one Mission church.

Midnight came and went. And then a boy, in his teens, stuck his head from the third-floor window and called down to the assembled crowds. He, like the others inside the building, was dressed all in white. "Nothing's happening!"

Inside the church some 1,000 followers had installed themselves while police barricaded the windows and the stairs connecting the building to the roof. This preventative measure was deemed necessary because the group was expected to take their lives as one, and authorities were tasked with stopping them, however they could.

The mayhem and disruption across the city of Seoul that night was the result of one man's actions, but by this point the man himself was in prison. His name was Lee Jang-rim, and he had predicted that 144,000 followers of his Dami Mission would enter the kingdom of heaven at midnight at the end of 28 October 1992. Those unfortunate enough to be left behind would, Lee stated, be embroiled in seven years of plagues, pestilence, war and famine. This in turn would bring about the Second Coming of Christ; when the Messiah arrived, all life on Earth would be utterly wiped out.

The Rapture, as it was described, is a key tenet of the Apostle Paul's letters in the Bible. At the End Times, he wrote, "We who are still alive and are left will be caught up" and will "meet the Lord in the air". When Jesus arrives from heaven, a trumpet will announce the rise of "the dead in Christ". The timing of Lee's prophecies was no coincidence. Beliefs in a coming apocalypse can be linked to the idea of new millennia; as a case in point, the Book of Revelation states that the Second Coming of Christ will usher in a new, 1,000-year reign of God's Son before the final judgement separates believers from non-believers.

South Korea is a largely Christian, conservative and traditional country, and Lee was able to persuade many of the veracity of his belief system. Many of his followers quit their jobs and sold their homes to be as ready as possible for the promised Rapture and their eternal lives in heaven. While the majority of adherents lived in South Korea, there were also branches of the cult observed in the United States. The Dami Mission had placed advertisements for new recruits in both the *Los Angeles Times* and *New York Times*. The publication of Lee's book – *Getting Close to the End* – also attracted new members. Many were highly educated and had previously worked in pressurized jobs in the government, media and elsewhere.

The timing of Dami Mission's popularity is interesting. During the late 1970s, the situation between North and South Korea was worsening. As we have seen, since the end of World War Two the peninsula had been divided and had installed two very different governments. In 1950, the Korean War raged between the two nations until concluding without a peace treaty, in 1953. In the years that followed, some came to regard the tensions between North and South Korea as the Second Korean War. Clashes erupted between them and, in 1976, two US Army officers were killed with axes by North Korean soldiers. On 29 October 1992, the *Los Angeles Times* reported that "Many South Koreans have expressed the desire for some form of divine certainty amid their country's rapid post-war change, its suddenly declining economy and continued political unrest". It was through this environment of fear and instability that the Dami Mission rose in popularity.

One woman, who had been trying to become pregnant for three years, terminated her seven-month pregnancy in the belief that she would not be lifted to heaven while carrying the weight of her baby. Such was the fear among Lee's followers that four other people took their own lives in the build-up to 28 October; another man had died two months earlier after fasting for around a month and a half at a Los Angeles-based Dami Mission. This latter incident was the precursor for widespread calls for the cult to be investigated and broken down.

As is so often the case, police were originally reluctant to intervene in the cult's activities and belief systems as the sanctity of freedom of religion prevented them from doing so. However, other churches began to criticize the radical beliefs of the Dami Mission and described it as blasphemous.

Just before the events that would come to define the doomsday cult, Lee was arrested and charged with fraud amounting to almost £350,000 of Church funds: the proceeds of his followers' "donations" to the Mission, which were to be used to purchase bonds that matured after the doomsday on 28 October. Other members were charged with passing out propaganda. From that moment, authorities carried out surveillance operations on particularly large Dami Mission congregations and their leaders.

Lee's Dami Mission translates as "preparing for the nearing future". Its message spread quickly around the country, with 166 different churches accepting his view that the world would end and a final judgement be enacted. During the height of its influence, the Dami Mission was provided as the reason for an influx of petitions for early discharge from soldiers, as well as deserters. These were people who wanted to leave and join Lee's movement.

Lee proclaimed that a boy of just 17, Ha Bang-ik, was the prophet who would provide the Mission and its devotees with the date of the world's end. According to Lee, it was Ha who informed him that 28 October would herald the End Times.

As the appointed hour came and went, those inside the Dami Mission churches grew increasingly distressed. One leader posited the theory that the delay could be explained by the fact that Israel, where the Rapture began, was 7 hours behind Korea. When 7 a.m. came and went, there was unrest. Believers began to leave the buildings, their heads down.

Lee would go on to apologise for the actions of his group while incarcerated and awaiting his trial. In December 1992 he was convicted of fraud and sentenced to two years in prison. After his release though, Lee changed his name to Lee Dap-gye and established a new church in Seoul's Mapo District. This new branch continued to proclaim Christ's Second Coming, but did not subscribe to the idea this will occur on a specific date. Ha, the posited Messiah, would later explain to the media that he was too young to have questioned the apocalyptic predictions and that, after the day passed without the Second Coming of Christ, he studied real theology out of repentance.

In 2011, years after his release, Lee continued to claim that the end of the world was approaching. Previous followers of the Dami Mission also maintain that apocalypse is imminent, but that this will take the form of new technology. One minister stated that doomsday would begin between 2013 and 2016, with microchips being installed in humans around the world to enable global access to personal data. Some even state that the beast described in the Book of Revelation bears a resemblance to one such chip.

NOTES FROM THE UNDERGROUND

The Russian Orthodox Church dates back to 988 CE, when the Grand Prince of Kiev was baptized by the Patriarch of Constantinople and the country subsequently became Christianized. While it shares much with other branches of the Christian Church, it has a different style of worship, believing that the Holy Spirit comes from God alone and not through Jesus Christ. It also rejects the primacy of the Pope found in the Catholic faith, believing instead that Jesus stands as head of the Church.

A new sect that split from the original Church emerged in the 1990s, named the True Russian Orthodox Church. Its leader was an engineer called Pyotr Kuznetsov, who began his "ministry" by writing books and embarking on tours of monasteries across Russia and Belarus.

Kuznetsov amassed followers largely through the idea that the Russian Orthodox Church was not conservative enough. As the years passed the following grew, particularly when he claimed that only members of his Church would be permitted to decide who went to heaven or hell. The group's use of the word "True" enabled it to both connect and distance itself from the umbrella religion from which it had stemmed, though it was also known as "Heavenly Jerusalem".

Little is known about Kuznetsov's early life, but he was originally from Belarus, and by the time he founded the sect he'd previously worked as an architect and was divorced. The group established itself in the village of Nikolskoye, a *selo* (small village) on Bering Island off the east coast of Russia. Initial reactions to the new arrivals were that they seemed eccentric but largely harmless, with members occasionally seen walking quietly through the streets in long black robes.

The group set up their new commune in abandoned houses and did not use any electricity. Kuznetsov also banned his followers from watching television or listening to the radio. They were forbidden from handling money and were told that credit cards, as well as the barcodes found on food wrappers, were Satanic.

Had the group continued along this odd but innocuous trajectory, it might never have come to light at all. Instead, October 2007 marked a turning point for Heavenly Jerusalem. It was then that 35 members of the cult, mostly women, burned their passports after Kuzentsov said the documents contained "the number of the beast" from Revelations: 666. They packed their few belongings and relocated from Nikolskoye to an underground cave nearby. "Local drunks had beaten up our men, and sworn at our women," Kuzentsov was said to have told the group. "Then God showed us the only path – to move underground."

It seemed that for the six weeks prior to the group's move, they had been working day and night to dig out and fortify their shelter, a man-made cave that was also described as a bunker built before the Russian Revolution, when it had been used primarily as a convent. A man of average height could just about stand up inside, and it had its own well, kitchen and rooms used by the cult's members for sleep and prayer.

They barricaded themselves inside and did not allow anyone else to enter. In fact, Kuznetsov stated that any attempt to remove them would result in mass suicide, as they would ignite their gasoline canisters and self-immolate.

Their aim was simple – to wait inside the hillside shelter for the end of the world. Kuznetsov had informed the group that this would occur in May 2008, and nothing could persuade them to emerge.

Priests from the original Russian Orthodox Church were asked to intervene but members of Heavenly Jerusalem refused to negotiate with them and fired their guns into the air. Archbishop Filaret, the senior Russian Orthodox cleric for the area, stated that only prayer and persuasion should be used to entice the group to leave and that he only wanted the group to return to normal Christian life. He also stated he was willing to wait until the group's stated day of reckoning in May, if necessary.

More attempts to coax the group out were conducted by rescue workers, doctors and even monks, but nothing could persuade the cult to come out. Communication was achieved through a small chimney pipe that poked out above the ground. The authorities were deeply concerned by this point, not least because there were four children inside the cave and one of them was 16 months old.

Kuznetsov was not actually inside the cave himself, as the leader had claimed to the group that God had set a different path for him. In November, he was arrested and charged with setting up a violent religious organization and disseminating books and pamphlets of an extreme nature. However, doctors determined he needed specialist treatment and Kuznetsov was remanded to a psychiatric facility.

The followers continued their campaign, though, and refused to leave. Oleg Melnichenko, the region's vice governor, maintained that, while there was no reason to storm the bunker, in the event of extreme weather conditions or other life-threatening events the authorities would have to act to save the lives of those inside. Emergency workers were sent to the site to try to ascertain how likely the cave was to flood or collapse.

Family members of those inside the cave were naturally distraught. Anna Vabishchevich recounted how her son, a 41-year-old man called Alexander, was holed up inside the bunker with his wife and two daughters. Alexander had, she stated, come under Kuznetsov's influence years before: "My son was kind and now he is mentally ill," she told the media. "It's like he is hypnotized."

The following March, a partial collapse occurred following heavy rain. Twenty-four of the group's members, now separated from the others, managed to escape. This was a huge relief to authorities, especially as four children were rescued. There were, however, at least ten others remaining.

By this point, tragically, two female followers had died: one from malnutrition caused by the fasting she had undertaken in preparation for the apocalypse, and the other from cancer. Their bodies had been buried in a hole but the hideous smells of decomposing flesh soon permeated the remainder of the dugout.

Meanwhile, Kutzetsov attempted to take his own life. He had been seen by a psychiatrist and in the wake of the discussion came to the realization that the world was not, in fact, headed for imminent destruction. He attempted to inflict terrible head injuries on himself using a wooden log and suffered terrible brain trauma as a result; he was then diagnosed as schizophrenic. He was later found unfit to stand trial.

In May, after the heavy snow that had blanketed the region began to melt, another collapse occurred. This time, emergency workers were able to gain access to the remaining members, and urged them to leave. "We could smell the stench through ventilation holes," said one local official. "As we pulled out the dead bodies, we suggested the others leave and they agreed."

It was clear that if they remained inside the cave, the remaining members of the group were likely to be poisoned by the fumes produced by the decaying bodies. The two dead women were exhumed and DNA tests were conducted to confirm their identities. The cave was then destroyed with explosives to prevent anyone else from entering it. The story had gathered speed and momentum, prompting authorities to worry that tourists might try to get inside.

Following their departure, the members were given a cow – they refused to take milk from cartons – and they regrouped in a prayer house in Nikolskoye. Following his release from the psychiatric facility, Kuznetsov joined them there. To this day, it is believed that Heavenly Jerusalem remains in the village.

THE HANDMAIDS' TALE

In 1973, a new organization called Prayer Group of the Rosary was established by Antonio Naccarato in Turin, Italy. Antonio came from a tiny village in Amantea in the south of the country and had worked in South America and France before settling in Turin, where he sold shoes on the streets of Piedmont. His was a tough, hand-to-mouth existence and faith was one of the few constants in his life.

The new group focused on the struggle between good and evil, and believed in Christ's Second Coming. The world according to Antonio was full of sin and needed absolution before the return of the Messiah. He could, he claimed, perform miracles and heal the sick.

Antonio's following grew with the involvement of another family member: his niece, Lidia. Like Antonio, she had been born into poverty and lived in Amantea until the age of 12. Her parents both worked as tenant farmers in the largely agricultural region until the sudden death of her father, who suffered an unknown accident at the age of 42. The remaining family members kept close ties with Uncle Antonio and he was known as a highly pious, charismatic figure. Following her father's death, Lidia moved to Turin to join her uncle along with her mother, sister and brothers. "We lived as if in the

Third World," she would later explain. "We had no radio, we never travelled by train, we only heard them in the distance from our house."

The move would likely have been slow and difficult for the family, and the differences between the southern town they had called home and northern Italy were stark. The north was and remains a richer, more expensive and more developed region of the country.

In 1972, Lidia was writing to a cousin based in the United States. It was at this point she purported to have seen a leaf settle on the paper, followed by gold writing. Words formed on the page and she watched in awe. "By finding this leaf you can save the Universe," it read. "To have eternal life and to give eternal life." The leaf itself, Lidia said, contained just the one word: her own name.

She informed her family members, and it was Antonio who provided the answer. Lidia was the connection between God, the Virgin Mary and all of humanity. He informed his niece that she alone could prepare the world for Christ's Second Coming and successfully vanquish the devil.

The Prayer Group of the Rosary took its teachings from the Bible, and in many ways it was not much removed from the Catholic Church. It did, however, also adhere to the mystical works of Maria Valtorta, who had written a text called *The Poem of the Man-God* and had died in 1961.

Over the following months, Lidia reported a series of visions that, it was interpreted, came from the Virgin Mary. As time went on members flocked to join the following, all of them firm believers in Lidia's prophetic power and many connected to the Naccarato family. Word of mouth appears to have been the primary means of recruitment to the cause. Followers now came from beyond Turin to marvel at Lidia's visions, with many making the journey of nearly 750 miles from Amantea, her birthplace.

Antonio Naccarato died in 1983, and his death was seen as a "sacrifice" for the cult's members, a necessary tribute in the battle against evil. "In an extreme gesture of love for all," Lidia described, "we made a resolution. In 1983, Uncle Antonio and I reciprocally offered our lives in sacrifice for the good of all, leaving it to God to determine the person who should die. On 7 June 1983 we knew that it had to be my uncle to die and for 40 days until his death he knew much suffering."

Group members began to wear only black and stopped going to dedicated churches for services and prayer meetings. Lidia claimed that the next years would bring an unspecified divine being to Earth, and a new prophecy would materialize. She also claimed that her uncle was sending her instructions and teachings from beyond the grave, one of which related to the End Times. The apocalypse would, Lidia stated, occur on 24 May 1988. At such time, her uncle would be resurrected alongside Jesus Christ.

At the beginning of 1988, Lidia announced a new system of hierarchy for the Prayer Group of the Rosary. Members were divided into groups – the Apostles of Life, the Consecrated, the Handmaids and the Little Virgins – based on their age and sex. By the end of the decade, followers numbered 1,000 and the group had established a headquarters at a farmhouse in Amantea.

A week before the apocalypse was scheduled, Lidia declared that Antonio had appeared to her and informed her that he would be resurrected the following day. Therefore, 18 May was proclaimed a day of prayer, with members eagerly anticipating the return of their former leader and founder. However, the day came and went with no sign of Antonio. In the wake of this terrible disappointment, Lidia stated that Antonio would arrive on 8 June. In the meantime, however, she gave more information. There was somebody within the cult, one of their own, who was plotting to kidnap and murder Lidia. Sent into a panic, the members armed themselves with rifles, knives and other weapons and prepared to fight this unseen, malevolent force. They dressed in multicoloured clothes and prepared for a joyful welcome for Antonio and the vanquishing of the unknown conspirator.

On 24 May, the original date of the apocalypse, Lidia informed her followers that Antonio had revealed the name of the evil person in their midst. His name was Pietro Latella, and he had been born in France but now lived in Turin. He was just 27 years old, and within the group he was known as one of the Consecrated.

Terrified, Lidia contacted her brother, Salvatore, and ordered him to gather the Consecrated, but to exclude the unfortunate Latella. Perhaps sensing something was wrong, Latella fled the group in his car, but was chased by former fellow members, who fired at his car until it crashed on the roadside. He was alive but had several fractured bones, so was taken back to the farmhouse and tied to a chair within a red circle that members painted on the floor. A cat was then sacrificed and members prayed in a circle. Latella was denounced as Judas Iscariot, the apostle said to have betrayed Jesus in the Bible, and 12 shots were fired to represent the number of apostles who joined Christ. Lidia claimed that Antonio had told her the only way to ensure the occurrence of the prophecies given thus far was through a human sacrifice.

Lidia lay down among her followers, dressed all in white and clutching a rosary, while they danced and sang around her as Latella slowly bled out. Some followers left the farmhouse to gaze at the night sky, awaiting the Second Coming, and reported a message in the stars that said "Viva Maria". They fired shots into the air, one of which even injured a member called Lorenzo Tomasicchio, who was taken to hospital.

When concerned medical staff asked how the injury had been sustained, the police were called and went to the farmhouse to investigate. On arrival, they found the front door welded shut. Forcing entry, to their horror they discovered Latella's body while members of the group continued to pray and dance in the background. They searched the entire estate and discovered cash and cheques equivalent to around £627,000, as well as numerous weapons and bullets. Members of the group were arrested. Lidia claimed she knew nothing about Latella or how he had died.

"We still don't know how much the Mafia and black magic were involved in this affair," said Luigi Belvedere, the investigating magistrate. While police continued their investigations Lidia was placed under house arrest; she was rearrested the following year and charged with having breached the terms of her confinement. She soon confirmed that Latella was murdered because he was in fact Satan, sent to thwart the Second Coming of Christ.

Lidia Naccarato was eventually placed in the San Luigi Gonzaga forensic hospital in Mantua. She was described as neat and clean, speaking calmly and dressed in long clothes. It soon became apparent, however, that Lidia was spending a great deal of time with another patient at the facility, who later became convinced she herself needed to pray to "save the world". Lidia was forbidden from attempting to convert or persuade other patients from that time on.

After this, members began to move away from the cult. No formal charges appear to have been made after Latella's death, while Lidia Naccarato's fate is foggy – she either remains at the psychiatric facility to which she was confined or has been successfully treated and rehabilitated. Reports suggest that a handful of Rosary supporters remained active even until as recently as 2010.

THE CRIME OF THE CENTURY

At a New Year's Eve party in 1968, a group of people at Barker Ranch listened spellbound as one man outlined an imminent apocalypse. Barker Ranch lies in California's Death Valley and was used as a storage space and small shop for miners between the 1940 and 1960s, when it was leased for commercial, domestic use. Access is incredibly challenging, with roads craggy and uneven and covered in rocks and boulders, but a small stream that dips down into the valley provides both drinking water and irrigation for vegetation. Electricity is provided by a windmill and a generator. Within the estate lies the Myers Ranch, a property of 40 acres owned by the Myers family.

The house's occupants had been staying at Myers Ranch for a few months. Their leader had met the granddaughter of the owners and the group was invited to stay there to use the space for an indeterminate amount of time.

This particular New Year's Eve party marked the first occasion the leader's followers had heard the phrase "Helter Skelter". The man was standing before them as they sat around a campfire, describing the racial conflict he knew was coming for the United States. He claimed to have had a vision in which Black men would no longer be able to date or marry white women. This had become more socially accepted since the desegregation laws of 1964 when the Civil Rights Act was passed.

Just eight months before the party, on 4 April 1968, Martin Luther King Jr had been assassinated. The outpouring of grief and rage and the rioting that followed his murder had seen the passing of the Civil Rights Act of 1968, which was signed into law on 11 April 1968. President Lyndon B. Johnson had described it as one of the "promises of the century".

At Myers Ranch, the group's leader stated that, in due course, Black men would retaliate when confronted with these dating curbs to their newly gained rights and crime rates would soar across California. Hideous acts of butchery were outlined as the man described the atrocities soon to befall the state and the wider country. White people would fight back, he said, and the war would escalate to the point that Black communities would murder all white and non-Black citizens.

Despite this horrific vision, the leader reassured his people they themselves had nothing to fear: when the apocalypse came, they would descend underground in Death Valley to wait out the turmoil. When it was all over, they'd emerge as the only white people left in the country, perhaps the world, and they would subjugate the Black people once and for all.

Just two months earlier, their leader had been listening to The Beatles. Their new double release was eponymously titled *The Beatles*, but soon became better known by its colloquial moniker, "the White Album". One of its songs was called "Helter Skelter". This, the man said, was proof of the war to come. One ex-follower would explain how he listened to the album incessantly, convinced that the true meaning of "Helter Skelter" was the story of the rise of Black people and the fall of the whites.

The group listening on that fateful New Year's Eve was called the Manson Family. Their leader was a man named Charles Manson.

Manson was born as Charles Milles Maddox in Cincinnati, Ohio, to 15-year-old Kathleen Maddox in November 1934. His father was likely Walker Henderson Scott Sr, who was nine years Kathleen's senior. When the teenager explained she was pregnant, he fled. Kathleen married William Eugene Manson while pregnant with her son, but the pair divorced three years later; Kathleen, it seemed, was often away from home on alcoholic binges with her brother Luther. The pair were both sentenced to prison in 1939 for assault and robbery.

The young boy was sent to live with his aunt and uncle in West Virginia, during which time, he later told a counsellor, the couple embarked on a highly religious phase with views bordering on the extreme. Manson rejoiced three years later when his mother was paroled. He frequently skipped school in his early years and later claimed to have set his school on fire at the age of nine. He was sent to the Gibault School for Boys in Indiana at the age of 13. This was the American equivalent of the British borstal system – in other words, a reformatory school. The school was run by Catholic priests, and Manson often ran away.

Manson committed his first crime at the age of 14 when he robbed a grocery shop after escaping Gibault. The following years represented a string of petty thefts and juvenile facilities. He was arrested multiple times and, following a car theft, he was sent to the National Training School for Boys in Washington, where it was discovered he was illiterate. This turbulence continued into his twenties with further crimes including rape, car theft, cashing forged cheques and pimping.

By 1967, Manson was 32 years old and had spent over 16 years of his life in various juvenile facilities and prisons. He moved to Berkeley in California, and it was here that the Manson Family was formed.

The majority of the cult's first followers were women and teenage girls, many of whom were emotionally vulnerable. Manson encouraged them all to take LSD and began a programme of total control and submission from which no follower was exempt. By the middle of 1968 he had around 20 highly devoted followers.

Those sat around the fireside on 31 December 1968 were horrified by what Charles Manson was telling them. But there seemed to be a means of salvation: Manson himself. The leader explained that they would never survive the coming race war on their own and they needed someone like him, a master, to guide them through the End Days. From this point onwards, the Manson Family began to prepare for Helter Skelter, the name of the apocalyptic scenario envisioned by Manson, filling cars with provisions and annotating maps that would enable them to escape to the deserts of Death Valley unscathed. The Manson Family also wrote and practised songs for an upcoming album that, they hoped, would kick-start the revolution. In the meantime, Manson would quote chapters from the Book of Revelation to his loyal followers. Aside from this section of the Bible, the Manson Family do not appear to have had other religious beliefs.

It was in early 1969 that Manson reportedly told followers that Helter Skelter would commence that summer; it was, he said, "ready to happen".

On 9 August 1969, the country awoke to headlines of murder and destruction. A group of Manson Family members had broken into a property in the wealthy Benedict Canyon neighbourhood of Los Angeles. There they had murdered five people, on Manson's instructions. The leader had instructed follower Tex Watson and three female members of the cult to go to 10050 Cielo Drive and kill whomever they found at the house. His one directive was that they be murdered "as gruesomely as you can".

In the previous months Manson had in fact visited the house, because its last tenant had been a music producer called Terry Melcher. Manson had been thrilled when Melcher considered his proposed album, but after allowing Manson to record a free demo at his studio Melcher had ultimately decided not to offer a recording contract. This thwarted Manson's mission to create and disseminate an album to rival The Beatles, and it is possible that he didn't know the house's occupants had recently moved out and new tenants had moved in. The group was indiscriminate on the night of the attacks. The first victim, Steven Parent, was just 18 and had been visiting the estate's caretaker. He was shot before the group even gained access to the house.

The four other victims were made to stand in the living room. A hairstylist called Jay Sebring, who worked mostly with Hollywood stars, was shot and stabbed to death. Wojciech Frykowski and his girlfriend Abigail Folger, a coffee heiress, were killed outside when they managed to flee the house. They had both been staying as guests of the final victim, the actress Sharon Tate.

Tate had gained fame through her 1967 film *Valley of the Dolls* and was married to the film-maker Roman Polanski, who was in Europe; Folger and Frykowski were staying with Tate in the meantime. At the time of her death, she was over eight months pregnant with their child. When the Manson Family members had finished their grisly task, the word "pig" was written on the front door in Tate's blood.

The People newspaper spared no detail in its 10 August edition in recounting the awful scenes police discovered at the house: "The red-haired, 26-year-old star, clad only in a bikini, was hanging by a white nylon rope looped over a beam in the ceiling of a room." Sergeant Stanley Klorman, one of the officers dispatched to the scene of the crime, said that there were clear signs of a struggle in the rooms of the house: "It looked like a battlefield up there," he stated. "In all my years, I have never seen anything like this before."

The following night, Manson joined his members on another murderous mission. He was, it was claimed, unhappy with the "messy" nature of the previous evening's crimes. The cult went to the home of Leno LaBianca, a grocery store executive, and his wife Rosemary on Waverly Drive, 12 miles east of 10050 Cielo. In the months before the Manson Family's attack they had reported missing items from the house and found their dogs, who had been left inside, outside the property. Manson and his followers had performed reconnaissance missions, it appeared, before their invasion on 10 August.

Leno and Rosemary were tied up and robbed before being stabbed to death. The words "Healter [sic] Skelter" were written on the walls in blood, as was "Rise" and "Death to Pigs". They were found the following day by Frank, Rosemary's 15-year-old son.

Los Angeles was horrified by the separate murders and the gruesome details only served to further charge the already terrible situation. Frykowski, for example, had been stabbed more than 50 times in what appeared to be a frenzy; he had also been shot twice. The public were appalled enough by the attack at 10050 Cielo Drive, but the subsequent slaughter of Leno and Rosemary proved the catalyst for widespread panic. What was more, there did not appear to be any connection between the two attacks besides their timing on consecutive nights and the fact that they had both taken place in Los Angeles. Police had believed initially that the first murders were committed in the process of a drug deal that had turned sour.

Nothing happened for several months, and, if it weren't for a subsequent car theft, the Manson Family might well have escaped justice for the gruesome murders. However, police were able to track the car to Barker Ranch. Around the same time, a female member of the cult, who was serving time for another murder of a former friend of Manson, told fellow inmates that she had been involved in what had become known as the Tate murders. Over the following eight weeks, all those involved in the crimes were arrested and charged.

The trial combined the murders of the five victims at Cielo Drive and the couple at Waverly Drive. It began in June 1970. One of the accused turned state's witness, and Manson arrived in court on the first day with the letter X carved into his forehead: this, he said, was a representation of the fact he had "X'd myself from your world". Three others cult members, Leslie Van Houten, Susan Atkins and Patricia Krenwinkel were tried alongside their leader. Other Manson Family members were excluded from the courtroom for being disruptive, but set up camp outside the courthouse, carved Xs into their own foreheads and claimed that if Manson was convicted they would set themselves on fire. When Manson shaved off all his hair, they followed suit.

Inside the court further drama erupted when Manson attempted to attack the presiding judge with a pencil and screamed that "somebody should cut your head off". From that moment onwards, the judge would bring a gun into the court's proceedings just in case Manson's next attempt was not thwarted quickly enough.

The ruling found all four guilty of murder in January 1971. They received the death penalty, which was later commuted in all cases to life in prison after the state of California outlawed capital punishment in 1972. The trial lasted some nine and a half months and was the longest capital trial in United States history, with the transcript covering over 30,000 pages.

MOVERS AND SHAKERS

The start of the sixteenth century represented a time of great social change across Europe. Martin Luther began to challenge the Catholic Church and its teachings from 1517, and the likes of John Calvin, Huldrych Zwingli and John Knox contributed to the debate in the years that followed across Scotland, Switzerland, Germany and other continental countries.

These were new, even heretical ideas at the time, which challenged preconceived ideas that the Catholic Church was the connective tissue binding God to His people. Specifically, Luther confronted the system of indulgences, whereby believers could purchase a pardon for their sins, and this in turn led others to investigate the rites and rituals of Holy Communion. Instead of a congregation dependent on priests and other "intermediaries" between God and humankind, what became known as the Protestant Reformation encouraged a more individualistic relationship that did not rely on the boundaries sanctioned by the Catholic Church.

Protestantism swept across England in 1534 after King Henry VIII's marriage to his Spanish wife, Catherine of Aragon, was annulled. Since the Pope would not grant him a dispensation for divorce, Henry created the Church of England, which combined elements of both Catholicism and Protestantism.

This in turn gave rise to new religious groups that aligned themselves as broadly Protestant or Catholic but with certain key differences dependent on the sect itself. One of these was the United Society of Believers in Christ's Second Appearing, known as the Shakers, which was founded in 1747. In that year, James and Jane Wardley broke away from the Quakers, another Protestant denomination, and formed what was then known as the Wardley Society in Bolton, north-west England. The couple claimed they received messages from God's spirits, often during religious ceremonies, and stated that the End Times were fast approaching.

Although little is known about the Wardley family's early lives, by the time they joined the Quakers, or Society of Friends, James worked as a tailor in Bolton and Jane likely did not work. They had little money. When Jane began to experience visions from God, she discussed the experiences with James and then with a wealthy merchant bricklayer called John Townley, who provided them with money to form the Wardley Society. Followers were soon entranced by the meditative silences that Jane would break with full bodily trembling, shaking, singing and screaming. In its earliest days of the group, the Wardleys amassed around 30 followers, all of them from Bolton. The couple soon moved to Manchester and more believers were gathered there.

The Shakers encouraged spiritual leadership roles for women, believing that Christ's Second Coming could only be achieved through a female figure. They espoused communal living and believed above all in the power of the Holy Spirit to manifest in their daily lives. They were also vehemently anti-war. Unusually for the time, they were vehemently against the racial inequality witnessed in England and the United States. For the Shakers, all men and women were equal, and the key to harmony was to prepare for the Second Coming while living as siblings in a self-sufficient, work-focused manner.

"Repent," Jane Wardley told her growing followers. "For the kingdom of God is at hand. And when Christ appears again, then all anti-Christian denominations – the priests, the Church, the pope – will be swept away."

Soon meetings were being held in the nearby cities of Manchester and Chester, but the Shakers were soon vilified for their novel forms of worship and their apocalyptic beliefs. Some were mobbed or even stoned.

One member was a small girl called Ann Lee, whose parents were both Shakers. Lee was born in Manchester in 1736 and worked in a cotton factory before marrying and having four children. Sadly, none survived childhood.

Lee soon began to describe the revelations she had experienced, particularly about the story of Adam and Eve and original sin. She confessed her sins to Jane and James and encouraged the group's followers to do the same. In 1770, she received a "manifestation of Divine light" and stated that she was the reincarnated Jesus Christ. From this moment onwards, Ann Lee was known as Mother Ann.

During the following years, Mother Ann was imprisoned on numerous occasions, most often on charges of blasphemy. Sundays were set aside for quiet contemplation and prayer but the Shaker habit of dancing and shouting soon paved the way for legal intervention. For Mother Ann, however, this was the only sure-fire way to bring the kingdom of heaven to Earth.

In 1774, Mother Ann and eight Shaker followers left Liverpool on the *Mariah* for what was then colonial America. Ann had received a vision of establishing a Shaker community there, too, but it is likely she was keen to be rid of the religious persecution she experienced in England.

The group's belief system was quickly adopted in their new home, specifically New York. Mother Ann described seeing "a large tree, every leaf of which shone with such brightness as made it appear like a burning torch, representing the Church of Christ, which will yet be established in this land." Named because of their often-frenzied behaviour during services, the Shakers were quite different from the more traditional umbrella religions.

When the American War of Independence erupted in 1775, Mother Ann and the Shakers supported neither the colonists nor the British; their pacifist nature made them a target among other armies, who regarded them as traitors.

One of the key tenets of the Shaker philosophy was its focus on communal living. All property was shared, with members persuaded to give up their belongings before moving into a Shaker settlement. Those outside the group were known as people from "the World". They were not, however, especially isolationist in the way of other cults described in these pages; visitors were permitted, most likely to encourage new recruits to join.

Members grew their own food and tended to the fields and plots around their communities for much of the day. Men and women were often segregated since Mother Ann had advocated the purity of a celibate lifestyle. Children were usually adopted but were given the option to leave the Shakers when they reached the age of maturity at 21.

Accompanied by her brother William, Mother Ann settled the first commune in Albany before beginning missionary work across Massachusetts and Connecticut. Her popularity and presence were aided by her oratorical skills and she was known to comment that the Shakers "are the people who turned the world upside down". This popularity was not ubiquitous, however, and in the Massachusetts town of Shirley, for instance, Mother Ann experienced the terror of mob violence. William and Ann subsequently died after one such attack: William in July 1783, and Ann in September of the same year.

Followers claimed, immediately after her death, that Ann was Christ incarnate and that, now she was gone, the Holy Spirit could be found "in all in whom the Christ consciousness awakens". To that end, perfection was the ultimate aim of all human endeavour. Between 1820 and 1860, the Shakers were extremely prevalent, with some 6,000 members, first on America's east coast then expanding to Indiana, Kentucky and Ohio. They became strongly associated with craftsmanship in furniture, and for music and songs. Manual labour – whether farming or crafting, singing or dancing – was seen as the Lord's work and a testament to the fervour of the believers' conviction that the kingdom of heaven was upon them.

During this time, Shaker clans in the south of the country started to free any Black slaves belonging to its congregation and often paid to release them. This period became known as the "Era of Manifestations", during which revelations and spontaneous dancing proliferated. As the contemporary historian William Hepworth Dixon noted in 1867: "Shakerism is a system which has a distinct genius, a strong organization, a perfect life of its own, through which it would appear to be helping to shape and guide, in no small measure, the spiritual career of the United States."

Despite its utopian ideals, Shakerism gradually tapered off from the mid to late nineteenth century in both the United

Kingdom and the United States. Since they were forbidden to have children and new recruits were not high enough in number to replace followers when they died, the Shakers' influence dwindled. By 1920, just 12 Shaker communities remained in the United States. One hundred years later, this figure was down to one.

A SUPPOSED SAVIOUR

China, 1952. Just three years previously the civil war had ended, bringing to a close the four-year conflict between the Chinese Communist Party (CCP) and the Kuomintang, or Nationalists, since the end of World War Two. Chairman Mao Zedong had created the People's Republic of China, and the United States had declared all ties with the communist country would be cut.

Mao's rule was one of control and he was a fierce proponent of insurgency, revolution and state ownership. Throughout the 1950s the country would undergo enormous social and economic change as agriculture and industry were collectivized. In 1952, the Five-anti Campaign began with the express purpose of preventing corruption: Mao targeted the wealthy, but no one was exempt from the encouragement to "denounce" a neighbour for intellectualism or "bourgeois" habits. It is believed that in Shanghai alone, from January to April 1952, almost 900 people took their own lives as a result of the brutal campaign.

A year earlier, Li Hongzhi was born in the north-eastern province of Jilin, which borders North Korea and Russia. Li's early years were unremarkable and after finishing school he worked on a stud farm before serving as a musician in the Jilin Provincial Forest Rangers Corps. Until 1991, his other jobs involved work in a guesthouse and as a security guard. But things changed in the early part of the new decade, when Li began to practise a movement he called Falun Gong.

Falun Gong was initially a combination of martial arts and Thai dancing that Li developed and later taught. This brought him a higher income stream than he was used to and soon he shifted his focus to treating disease and "exerting his gong energy potency". Soon, Li's name became synonymous with mystical healing powers more successful by far than anything Western medicine could offer. Falun Gong's main objective seems to have been advocating for personal and mental "fitness", and his consultations and speaking engagements, during this time, amassed him a considerable fortune.

Li gave frequent lectures, travelling far and wide. His teachings were soon collected in a book called *Zhuan falun*; this was translated into nine languages, and in English is known as *The Revolving Dharma Wheel*. Here, Li called on his followers to meditate, follow a wholesome and healthy lifestyle and attempt to achieve spiritual enlightenment. It was at this point that Li began to introduce ideas of doomsday to his growing congregation. Followers of Falun Gong, he said, would be the only ones to "reach consummation and ascend to heaven".

Human beings, he claimed, had little time left on the planet and would soon be extinct. He decried modern science and claimed that the apocalypse was coming, destruction was inevitable and only he as the saviour of his people could save trusted followers. More concerning for the CCP was Li's notion that the government was ineffective and that only Falun Gong could effectively solve the issues facing the world.

After the book's publication, Li explained to his followers that he was no longer a mere "master" of healing and supernatural powers, but "the greatest Buddha of the universe". His followers were now firmly of the opinion that he could move objects with his mind, become invisible, read both the past and the future and even perform mind control. For an ever-widening group of people, Falun Gong was the perfect method of escaping the worries and pressures of everyday life in a country that had witnessed terrible famines, mass paranoia, riots, denouncements, exiles, murders and suicides. As time went on and members who became ill refused traditional medical help, some died, while others took their own lives or the lives of others to reach "Consummation".

Any dissent or challenge to the Falun Gong movement was met with fierce rebuttal by followers: scholars and journalist were mobbed by followers and clashes became more frequent. In 1996, for example, the *Guangming Daily*, a state-run newspaper, published a piece that claimed Falun Gong was nothing more than a "pseudo-science" that was conning thousands of people; members of the group then began a campaign of letter writing to the publication.

Li next began the process of cementing his movement in the national consciousness, using the wealth he'd accumulated to establish the Falun Dafa Research Society, of which he was president, and set up 39 general stations across the country.

In the mid-1990s, Li announced his work in China was done and left to recruit new followers to the practice of Falun Gong. In 1997, he was awarded honorary American citizenship in recognition of his contributions to spiritual and physical health, and moved to New York the following year.

By 1999, the movement had grown exponentially, with about 100 million global practitioners of Falun Gong. This figure can be taken with a pinch of salt, since Li himself offered the number, but what is certain is that the number was substantial. In April 1999, 10,000 members of the Falun Gong clan were involved in a huge demonstration in Zhongnanhai, a compound for the CCP's top leaders. They were there to request official recognition for the group but the protest shook Chinese authorities and the CCP's general secretary, Jiang Zemin, ordered the group to disband.

By July 1999, Falun Gong was banned. At this point, it is believed, over 1,400 people had died from practising it in a variety of different ways, often by refusing to seek medical treatment when it was required, as Li was believed to have the power to cure all ailments. Jiang called it an "evil cult".

Of course, Li was nowhere near China when this unfolded, particularly since Jiang had ordered a warrant for his arrest. Over the months that followed, thousands of Falun Gong supporters were arrested and Li's books were seized and destroyed. The cult had been outlawed.

This did little, however, to stop its rise. Li's followers continued their practice even while many of their number were thrown into prison and tortured after sham trials. The CCP claimed that Falun Gong had "engaged in illegal activities, advocating superstition and spreading fallacies, hoodwinking people, inciting and creating disturbances, and jeopardizing social stability".

Li attempted to engage the CCP in discussions about the future of Falun Gong but the government was unrelenting. Its leaders had only to look to recent history to see the trouble and strife religiously motivated rebellions could cause them:

in the nineteenth century, the Taiping Heavenly Kingdom had even attempted to oust the country's emperor. In addition, the CCP was more than aware that its ideologies and belief system were utterly incompatible with organized religion. Mao's tyrannical leadership had instigated state atheism when the CCP first took power and any new groups were viewed with deep suspicion.

The CCP then launched a new body called the 610 Office (named for the day it was formed: 10 June 1999) whose sole purpose was to capture and "re-educate" the followers of Falun Gong. From the media to police and the army, the campaign was bolstered by news reports and radio announcements. Many members were sent to forced labour camps, had their organs harvested or were sent to psychiatric facilities without a hope of ever emerging. So severe was the perceived threat that the 610 Office – otherwise known as the Central Leading Group on Preventing and Dealing with Cults – was only formally dissolved in 2018.

The Falun Gong responded with the creation of a free newspaper called *The Epoch Times*, as well as underground television and radio broadcasts. Over the following years, however, and with no sign of their leader, members began to turn away from the group. Whatever doomsday might bring, it was nothing compared to the punishment they would receive here on Earth for participating in the movement.

While China has demanded Li's extradition from the United States, he has remained there ever since. In 2001, he was awarded an International Religious Freedom Award at the Senate, and he was nominated for the Nobel Peace Prize in 2000 and 2001.

A MOTLEY CREW

Born in 1931, Marshall Applewhite was the son of a Presbyterian minister and grew up in the city of Spur, Texas. His childhood was characterized by strong religious beliefs and he attended Christian schools before going on to read philosophy at college. Afterwards, he studied theology at the Union Presbyterian Seminary, married and had two children.

The first 40 years of Applewhite's life were quietly unremarkable. Not long after beginning his seminary career, he decided to switch paths and focus on music instead. He was a baritone singer and worked at a Presbyterian church in North Carolina, where he was employed as the music director.

From 1948 until 1973, the United States had a policy of compulsory military service, and in 1954 Applewhite was drafted into the Army Signal Corps, serving in Austria and New Mexico. His army career lasted two years until he left and enrolled at the University of Colorado, gaining a master's degree in music.

By the early 1960s, Applewhite was living in New York and auditioning for musical theatre roles. Despite his impressive voice and stage presence, these attempts did not prove especially fruitful and he was next found at the University of Alabama running the student choirs. The family's next move was to Texas, to the University of St Thomas in Houston. He was subsequently fired because, it was alleged, he had been conducting a relationship with a male student. At this point he found himself divorced and struggling. Nothing had seemed to work out how he'd planned it to, and all the moving, studying and auditioning had come to nothing.

The social stigma attached to homosexuality was high. Most US states had not yet decriminalized same-sex relations, and Texas, the last state to do so, didn't enact such legislation until 2003. Applewhite checked into a psychiatric hospital around this time as, according to later reports, he was seeking to be "cured" of homosexual desires.

At the hospital, Applewhite met Bonnie Nettles, a married nurse who had a keen interest in biblical prophecies. Their connection was immediate and strong; Nettles explained that their meeting had been predicted by aliens from another planet and Applewhite was convinced he must have known Bonnie in a previous life. Soon enough, Applewhite and Nettles declared themselves the two witnesses described in the Book of Revelation and set off around the country. Their first follower was a woman called Sharon Morgan, who left her children to join the pair but returned a month later. During this time Applewhite and Nettles stole a rental car and were arrested for credit card fraud (using Morgan's accounts) in 1974. Although the fraud charges were dropped, Applewhite was remanded in jail for six months before being released and continuing his missionary work with Nettles.

Their burgeoning philosophy appears to have been a mixture of biblical prophecy, particularly concerning the doctrine of the "last things" or Second Coming of Christ, millennialism and science fiction, such as the books of Arthur C. Clarke. They wrote a pamphlet describing how Jesus had been reincarnated as Applewhite himself, who was the "Present Representative" of Christ. They claimed that they would one day be killed, resurrected and leave Earth on a spaceship. This event, when it occurred, would be known as "the Demonstration".

The pair's movement grew as they advertised their meetings and promised anyone who joined ascension to a higher level of evolution. By 1975 the group had around 25 members and was growing fast. In September of that year, the pair preached at a motel hall in Oregon and successfully convinced 20 people to sell their goods and cut ties with their families. The *CBS Evening News* even reported on the mysterious vanishing act: "A score of persons... have disappeared," said the anchor Walter Cronkite. "It's a mystery whether they've been taken on a so-called trip to eternity – or simply been taken."

This increased focus on the group and its activities panicked both Applewhite and Nettles. They did not want mass media attention. The group left mainstream society at this point and set off into the countryside: "the crew" camped most nights and were forced to beg for money in the streets. Concerned family members of the cult's followers attempted to track them down but their itinerant lifestyle made this more challenging.

Applewhite and Nettles also ensured total loyalty to their cause by expelling members they didn't feel were committed enough, which in turn created the dependence and obedience they desired. Recruitment did continue and at the height of its activities the group had over 200 members. In 1976, they stopped recruiting.

Smoking and drinking were forbidden, as was sex. Some male followers were castrated in order to curb their libido; Applewhite himself was believed to have undergone the surgery. Gender was seen as a distraction and so members were forced to wear baggy clothes and keep their hair short. Any attachment to the planet through possessions, clothes, books, pets, loved ones or jobs was seen as a negative.

In the early 1980s the cult settled in several different houses and appeared to have stopped travelling on the road. Then came bad news: in 1985, Bonnie Nettles died of cancer, devastating the movement. How could this have happened to their messenger on Earth and why had she not been taken by extraterrestrials, as promised? Applewhite, despite his grief, hurried to convince them that Nettles' consciousness had merely quit her physical, earthly body. This was, in figurative terms, what had been foretold when it was predicted that her body would leave the planet in a UFO.

Until the end of the decade, Applewhite's group continued, though in a more muted fashion. Once the shock of his partner's death had abated somewhat, however, Applewhite encouraged his followers to begin their mission once more. They made a series of videos that were widely broadcast, called *Beyond Human – The Last Call,* and Applewhite proclaimed the end of the world was imminent. At the dawn of the digital age, the group set up a website that spread the message of doomsday more widely. In time, the cult formed a sophisticated computer business and earned a great deal of money from the work its members did.

In 1995, the astronomers Alan Hale and Thomas Bopp discovered a new comet, which became known as Comet Hale–Bopp. For 18 months, the incredible sight was visible without a telescope. Applewhite was fascinated by the comet and believed it provided the secrets of his group's salvation. The phenomenon represented, according to the group, the approaching spaceship (which was hidden behind the comet) that would take them to the kingdom of heaven. This was their last chance to evacuate Earth.

By this point the cult was living at a large, expensive house it called "the Monastery" in Rancho Sante Fe in California. On 19 March 1997 Applewhite recorded a video in which he explained mass suicide was the only means to achieve evacuation before the gates of heaven closed forever. Although the crew had been opposed to the concept of suicide, the definition of the word was reworked to suit their purposes: now, it was described as turning "against the Next Level when it is being offered". This prompted the idea that *not* taking their lives was in fact the traditional method of suicide, while their own actions were vehicles of salvation.

On 21 March, 38 followers joined Applewhite at a restaurant for a "last supper" in which everyone ordered the same meal – turkey pot pie, cheesecake with blueberries and iced tea – before returning to the house. Each member recorded their own farewell message, dressed in black shirts and Nike Decade shoes, before the suicides began to take place.

The group's website was updated for the final time:

> *By the time you read this, we suspect that the human bodies we were wearing have been found and that a flurry of fragmented reports have begun to hit the wire services... The task was not only to bring in information about that Evolutionary Kingdom Level Above Human but to give us the experience of working against the forces of what the human evolutionary level, at this time, has become.*

Over the following days there were three waves of death: each member of the crew drank a solution of phenobarbital mixed with apple sauce and vodka. Their identical armbands read "Heaven's Gate Away Team". Just before the last set of suicides, the videotaped farewell messages were sent out to affiliated members of the cult and to the BBC. Upon receipt of these tapes, the Sheriff's Department in San Diego was alerted, but by the time the deputy arrived at the Monastery it was too late.

There were 39 bodies at the house: 21 women and 18 men, all between the ages of 26 and 72. They had died over the course of the past days in groups of between nine and 15. It was determined that Applewhite had been one of the very last to die.

Alan Hale, one of the men who discovered the comet, later described how he had known, long before the events of what was later called Heaven's Gate, that there would be repercussions. "We are probably," he told a colleague at the time, "going to have some suicides as a result of this comet... The sad part is that I was really not surprised. Comets are lovely objects, but they don't have apocalyptic significance. We must use our minds, our reason."

In the months following the grisly events of spring 1997, other former members of the group took their lives in manners similar to those used by the crew. One suicide note, left by a 58-year-old man from California, claimed he too was leaving on the spaceship. To this day, the Heaven's Gate website is live, though it has not been updated since the mass suicide, which marked the end of its activities. The original slogan at the top of the page still reads "Red Alert".

FINAL WORD

There is nothing so enticing, and yet so dangerous, as groupthink. The stories recounted in this book reveal the extent of human willingness to belong, to feel a sense of connection, to quest for something beyond the mundane. This propensity to follow, to dedicate years or even a lifetime to a specific cause, has been revealed the world over: as ubiquitous in its potential in sub-Saharan Africa, the deserts of Australia, a bustling European metropolis or a remote Asian jungle.

There is nowhere, therefore, that is immune to the allure of a new method and manner of living. Where there are humans, we must assume, so too will there be offshoots of supposed "normality", fringe groups where often outlandish, outrageous or downright frightening ideas are left to propagate like weeds.

Some of the cults outlined in these pages have advocated for a retreat from the world: members have shed their worldly ties, possessions and financial responsibilities to enter a more monastic, frugal state of living. Of course, rejection of the societal norms and expectations designed to protect a population – whether that be through policing, healthcare resources, education or housing – comes with its own issues when a cult becomes myopic, when it sets its own rules and enters its members into a bondage that proves almost impossible to escape. Other groups have taken more overt, public action, attempting to bring others to their cause through campaigns, acts of terrorism, vandalism and political sabotage.

Perhaps the most frightening of all are those that advocate for the ultimate sacrifice, the doomsday groups of our last chapter that have so thoroughly convinced themselves of a certain doctrine that death appears the only rational course of action. At the heart of all such groups lie seemingly benevolent but often deeply misguided leaders who exploited the fears, worries and anxieties of members for their own ends. Many of these ordinary people have experienced the horrors of financial, physical and sexual abuse at the hands of leaders and their inner circles. All too often, the relevant authorities were almost powerless to investigate or prevent the crimes committed under the cloaks of these cults, as laws enshrining religious freedoms proved the barrier to justice.

What becomes most clear, perhaps, through these stories is the propensity of cults and sects to flourish in times of great political or socio-economic upheaval. Where there is poverty, mistrust of elected leadership, natural disaster and polarized opinion, one can almost guarantee the establishment of groups designed to offer an alternative.

But these tales are not, unfortunately, consigned to the past. With the rise of social media and its cultish following, fake news stories, conspiracies and misconceptions entrap millions in their pursuit of community and information. The stories in this book are more than insights into the strangest and most shocking cases over the world and across time: they are, and should remain, a lesson for the future.

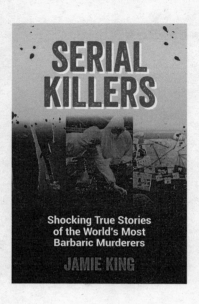

SERIAL KILLERS

Shocking True Stories
of the World's Most
Barbaric Murderers

Jamie King

ISBN: 978-1-83799-122-8

TRUE CRIME STORIES

Shocking Tales of Real-Life
Murderers, Thieves,
Con Artists and Gangsters

Jamie King

ISBN: 978-1-83799-007-8

UNSOLVED MYSTERIES

Unexplained Events and
Paranormal Phenomena
from Around the World

Jamie King

ISBN: 978-1-80007-990-8

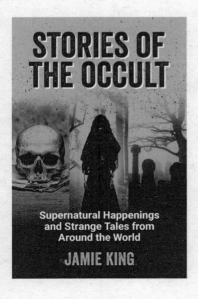

STORIES OF THE OCCULT

Supernatural Happenings
and Strange Tales from
Around the World

Jamie King

ISBN: 978-1-80007-934-2

Have you enjoyed this book?
If so, why not write a review on your favourite website?

If you're interested in finding out more about our books,
find us on Facebook at **Summersdale Publishers**, on
Twitter/X at **@Summersdale** and on Instagram and
TikTok at **@summersdalebooks** and get in touch.
We'd love to hear from you!

Thanks very much for buying this Summersdale book.

www.summersdale.com